Praise for SELECT SELLING

Selling is a perennial challenge for firms in technologically-intensive industries and many firms fail because they mismanage the selling process. **SELECT SELLING** provides a pragmatic and contemporary guide to selling, its pitfalls and how they can be overcome. A very useful book.

WALTER KUEMMERLE
Associate Professor, Harvard Business School

What impresses me about **SELECT SELLING** is that it addresses the problem of sales and strategic marketing synergy heads-on. And until companies deal with this in a pragmatic way, there will always be the "chasm" between the two groups. **SELECT SELLING** shows you how to bridge that gap.

MARK CAVENDER
Founder and Managing Director, Chasm Institute LLC

We have used **SELECT SELLING** here at Expedia. Being able to put the tools to work by giving the worksheets to the sales people is extremely valuable. Everyone should use the qualification models, questioning techniques, and sales planning tools that are provided in this book. It helps you grow revenue fast. It has certainly helped me manage the national sales team.

PATRICIA C. ELLIOTT
Senior Vice President, Expedia Corporate Travel

A most enjoyable read – It's great! An interesting mix of practical take-aways, plus good discussion/case history from real-life examples. Tools, worksheets, and examples are a great idea; I think this is the key thing – you can read the theory, hear about an example, but then grab one of the sheets and start doing it for your own business.

SEAN O'SULLIVAN
CEO, Rococo Software

This book should be in the hands of every professional sales executive who wants to stay at the top of their game. The experience of the authors is obvious as you read it. They have clearly been out there doing it. It's a **must** read for any twenty-first century sales professional.

BARRY HORN
CEO, Liberty Financial Group

I wish I had **SELECT SELLING** at the start of my career. It's straightforward and pragmatic. Buy it, read it, and most of all, use it.

JOHN WALL
CEO, Vista.com

SELECT SELLING is a very timely book. Getting highly-paid salespeople in a high-tech environment to be focused, efficient with their time and, ultimately, to be successful is a constant challenge for executives. This is the best book I have read to date that addresses these issues. It merges expert, yet practical, advice with very useful worksheets and templates. I have already gained a lot of benefit from reading this book. It is also an excellent read. It is a book that I know I will refer to many times in the next few years and will certainly refer all our salespeople to it.

BARRY MURPHY
CEO, Netsure

The experience encapsulated in **SELECT SELLING** is invaluable. I want my sales team to read this right away. It's a very enjoyable read. The content is well-presented and the tools are clearly based on years of selling experience.

LIAM MULLANEY
Managing Director, Sage Ireland

It's a fine book. The language used is easy and friendly. It's great to have the theory, the case studies and the worksheets, all in one place. I look forward to being able to buy a copy for each of the sales people in System Dynamics.

TONY McGUIRE
CEO, System Dynamics

SELECT SELLING is a roadmap for successful selling. It is easy to read and packs a lot of crucial advice. The tools and worksheets are very well constructed to be usable by a salesperson in the daily sales grind. I would recommend it to anyone selling complex products.

GERRY ENGLISH
Regional Sales Manager, Misys PLC

This book addresses the real issues faced by sales executives who are in the front-line every day. The theory is there, but the examples and worksheets make it an essential companion. I would recommend this to any sales person selling to large corporations.

JOHN NOLAN
CEO, PixAlert

Securing sales and growing repeatable quality revenues is the biggest challenge facing young high-technology companies today. **SELECT SELLING** provides pragmatic advice and easy-to-use frameworks that the leaders of these companies, both CEOs and Sales Vice Presidents, can use to conquer the sales and revenue challenge.

SHAY GARVEY
General Partner, Delta Partners

SELECT SELLING

STRATEGIES TO WIN CUSTOMERS BY DEFINING THE ULTIMATE TARGET PROFILE & DISCOVERING WHAT THEY REALLY WANT

Donal Daly
Paul O'Dea

www.oaktreepress.com

OAK TREE PRESS
19 Rutland Street, Cork, Ireland
www.oaktreepress.com

A catalogue record of this book is
available from the British Library.

ISBN 1-86076-297-2

Printed in Ireland by ColourBooks.

CONTENTS

FIGURES

ACKNOWLEDGMENTS

An undertaking like this book is beyond the capacity of the authors alone. At each step along the way, we received extraordinary support and guidance from a broad constituency of contributors and reviewers. At the core of the book is the **SELECT SELLING** methodology, which owes its value to our customers across the globe. It is through their implementation experience that we have been able to refine the **SELECT SELLING** tools and models, to reflect what works, and what doesn't. Every time a company uses **SELECT SELLING**, we learn more about the dynamics of selling complex products. We are constantly impressed by the wisdom of the experienced sales professionals we have been privileged to work with, and are grateful for their tenacity and insights. We hope we have captured some of the value they shared with us.

We wanted to be sure, when writing this book, that it would not be just another sales book. We mined the experience of the attendees of the SalesSTAR program, an education initiative for CEOs of technology companies, in which we are involved. The value derived from these practitioners was immense. The SalesSTAR CEOs shared their experiences, and helped us to refine the **SELECT SELLING** methodology as it pertains to both the strategic and execution issues inherent in the sales process.

In this book, we were joined in true partnership by our supporters and sponsors, who were many. In particular, we are indebted to:

- Inter*Trade*Ireland – the all-island trade and business development body, who are working in collaboration with both the Irish Software Association and Momentum, and are sponsoring the publication of this book as part of their strategy of facilitating all-island business networks
- Ronan Daly Jermyn – a rare breed of commercial savvy pragmatic lawyers

- Delta Partners – a progressive venture capital firm, focused on technology companies
- FÁS – the training and employment authority – for its constant and valued support
- The Irish Software Association – in some ways, our *alma mater* – and Momentum – its counterpart in Northern Ireland
- Enterprise Ireland – who show uncanny vision for company development.

For their support, and belief in the project, we are truly grateful.

We are keen to acknowledge the many professionals, sales, marketing, and technology advisors and practitioners, who took time out from their busy schedules to share their opinions and comments with us. We list them here in alphabetical order: Tammy Billington, Mark Cavender, Brian Caulfield, Mischelle Davis, Patti Elliott, Gerry English, Pat Frain, Cathal Friel, Shay Garvey, Pat Gibbons, Barry Horn, Ian Hyland, Gerry Kelly, Margaret Kennedy, Walter Kuemmerle, Tony McGuire, Patricia McLister, Liam Mullaney, Barry Murphy, John Nolan, Sean O'Sullivan, Kathryn Raleigh, Aidan Stack, and John Wall.

In **SELECT SELLING**, we have tried to encapsulate the best of our experience, and improve it with the wisdom of those mentioned above. Any shortcomings or mediocrities are ours alone.

As we toiled to complete this project, many nights and weekends that should have been spent with our families were spent instead creating, writing and revising. We are grateful for the unquestioning support of Cleona, Robin, Christian, Clare, Sean, Maria and Ross. This book is for them.

Thank you.
Donal Daly
Paul O'Dea

Sponsored by

FOREWORD

Ask a sales representative why they lost the deal, and inevitably the blame will fall on marketing:

> "They didn't tell product management what features are needed in the product. The leads they give us are no good. Our collateral and website stinks. Our demos are boring and don't show our strengths. And, we get absolutely no good press or analyst coverage."

Now ask marketing why the sales force is behind quota and loses more deals than it wins:

> "We add new features to the product, but they can't explain them. We generate leads, but they won't follow up on them. We create great sales collateral and have a state-of-the-art website, but prospective customers never see either. They don't know how to demo the product. They won't quote us when we're given favorable press and analyst coverage."

Stop! You're both right! Or, perhaps, you're both wrong! As a former sales rep, a former marketer, and now a consultant and educator, I have definitely been on both sides of the fence.

Backtrack to 1986. I came off a great year selling software with a major applications software company. In fact, I was named "Territory Manager of the Year" for 1985. After my ego recovered, I was asked to give a presentation to the marketing team at headquarters. They wanted (seriously!) to know what they could do to help the sales force be more effective. I asked a question: "How many of you have ever been with a representative on a sales call?". Out of a group of 35 marketing people, no hands went up. So much for marketing understanding what sales needs.

Now fast-forward to the present day. As a Managing Director for The Chasm Group for 10 years, and now as Founder and Managing

Director of Chasm Institute LLC, I've had the privilege of working with and advising over 200 companies. And yes, there is a common thread: sales and marketing are *not* in sync. That's where **SELECT SELLING** comes in. I've seen lots of sales training programs, and read lots of books about selling. And let me say that I've learned something in each and every one of them. But what impresses me about **SELECT SELLING** is that it addresses the problem of sales and strategic marketing synergy heads-on. And, until companies deal with this in a pragmatic way, there will always be the "chasm" between the two groups. **SELECT SELLING** shows you how to bridge that gap.

SELECT SELLING addresses the fundamental issue of choosing your leaping-off point – selecting your target customer. That's where strategic marketing converges with the best of professional selling. It's like having a chasm-crossing philosophy at an individual customer level. Rich in strategic advice, yet coupled with practical 'here's how to do it' tools and worksheets, **SELECT SELLING** extends principles of segmentation first written about in *Crossing the Chasm* into the sales organization.

Donal Daly and Paul O'Dea provide an informative, easy-to-read view of what it really takes to be successful in high-tech sales. The book is full of practical ways of selling in today's tough business environment. And, it addresses the tough issue of the "chasm" between sales and strategic marketing. Cross *this* chasm, and your company will be well on its way to success.

Mark Cavender
Founder and Managing Director, Chasm Institute LLC

CHAPTER 1

WHAT IS SELECT SELLING?

There are few distinct viewpoints in business that are as polarized as those of marketing and sales professionals. Marketing is glamorous, sales less so. Sales are measurable, marketing less so. The uneasy relationship between sales and marketing is widespread and infects almost all types of businesses, particularly technology companies that provide high value solutions to large corporations. Marketing folks decry the poor sales conversion rate delivered by the sales team, who in turn abhor what they would characterize as the risible value delivered by expensive marketing campaigns.

During the production of this book, we interviewed many sales and marketing professionals. The polarity of perspective was striking. "Sales people are just quick-talking, quota-driven snake oil dealers" was the cant of the marketing quarter, while the sales constituency responded, "Sales draw the picture and marketing color it in!"

Like many opposing forces, however, their true interdependence is understated and sometimes unclear. The strategic marketing function (not marketing communications) believes that it sets out the game-plan, sometimes only to find that there are no players who understand the strategy. Sales execute plays, without understanding where the corporate goal is. On today's playing field, successful selling, and the leading sales professional, encapsulates the best of strategic marketing, but at an individual customer level. Today's sales winners eschew their previous role as vehicles for value *communication* and take responsibility for value *creation*, delivered to carefully chosen prospects – to convert them to customers.

Principles, once seemingly engraved in stone, now reveal themselves to be more fluid than rigid. In a world where 'value creation' is a necessity, and the foundation upon which profitable sales relationships are built, activity alone no longer suffices. The old adage of 'sales is a numbers game' rings hollow in a world where information is everywhere, and customers are frequently as knowledgeable as you are about your products, and those of your competitor. Unless you create – rather than just communicate – value, customers will look elsewhere. Professional selling has evolved beyond a "Go get 'em, Tiger!" approach, and a good listener will beat a fast talker anytime. Customers now look to a sales professional to be their partner in developing a future vision for their organizations. They expect actions – not just words. The winning professional salesperson[1] is becoming a customer confidante, a **trusted advisor** in his industry, and the person who leads his colleagues to President's Club, year after year.

THE SELECT SELLING METHODOLOGY

The SELECT SELLING methodology has been designed against this evolving background. Its function is to equip anyone selling high value, complex products to large corporations with a defined and rigorous process that can be molded to an individual salesperson's style but which also takes much of the uncertainty out of the sales process. It combines high-level, strategic marketing principles to draw the map, with focused tactics to complete each journey, addressing the practical stops along the way.

The purpose behind the book is to help you grow revenue. We have all spent too many hours in airports, traveling to sales calls, to focus on anything else. Selling is an honorable profession – but a tough one. Rejections are many and varied, and there are as many highs as lows. But when it's good, when you close that big deal, or win a really competitive bid, there is almost nothing to compare.

We have defined a repeatable sales process that is pragmatic and usable. It's not overloaded with paperwork. The SELECT SELLING process (see **Figure 1**) sets out key principles, and arranges them into a series of six manageable, actionable steps – a framework that you can adopt to aid your efforts:

---

1 Though we see an equal balance of high performers between the genders, we use the masculine pronoun throughout the book, rather than force the reader through multiple 'he or she', or 'his or her', references.

1. Select Target Customer.
2. Understand Buyer Need.
3. Qualify the Opportunity.
4. Plan and Manage the Pipeline.
5. Execute the Sales Plan.
6. Negotiate and Close.

FIGURE 1: THE SELECT SELLING PROCESS

SELECT SELLING will be of particular value to those in the high technology industry. It will help you enhance your productivity, hit your targets more consistently, and increase revenue. We were aided in the structure and final definition of the methodology by many world-class sales professionals; shaping, nudging and tweaking, to help us create a complete and cohesive set of practical and executable models. Applied in organizations large and small, the models used in **SELECT SELLING** are truly tried and tested, and have been proven successful time and again. Where **SELECT SELLING** is adopted, focused activity becomes the norm, sales forecasts are more accurate, and revenue increases. Where SELECT SELLING is adopted throughout the supporting functions of marketing, service and operations, an uncommon organizational alignment is achieved, resulting in true team-based selling.

Select means many things. According to Merriam Webster, it means 'chosen from a number or group by fitness or preference'; it means 'of special value or excellence: exclusively or fastidiously chosen often with regard to social, economic, or cultural characteristics'; and it means 'judicious or restrictive in choice'. In the context of SELECT SELLING, it means all of these things. It is about efficiency, spending time only where it's worthwhile, choosing the customers that are more likely to buy, and controlling your destiny as a sales professional. Underlining this methodology is a belief that professional selling is – first and foremost – professional. You are a 'trusted advisor' for your customers, working on the right opportunities, and closing more deals. Professional salespeople generate more revenue for their companies and make more money for themselves. SELECT SELLING is about professional selling. In the end, it all comes down to you. In **Chapter 2: How to Become a Sales Specialist**, we suggest a way to raise your game, and maintain that position at the higher echelon of your profession.

Select the Customer

Few companies have products that truly appeal equally to broad horizontal markets – and very few companies ever went out of business for being too focused. Concentrating exclusively on those customers whose needs mirror the advantages and benefits you offer is critical to efficiency. Making choices means that you must exclude some opportunities. You must ignore markets where the fit of customer requirements to your offering is not absolute. Only where the wheels of your engine mesh smoothly with the cogs of the customer's power plant should you expend energy. This is your 'sweet spot'. It's where all the forces align. The benefit you deliver to your customer is extreme. Adequate, but not extravagant, resource is expended to acquire the customer. Profitability increases. Customer satisfaction is high, and the conversion rate of prospect to customer is greater than the norm.

Companies struggle to choose the companies they should pursue for business. In many cases, the irrational fear of potential missed opportunities drives otherwise rational sales and marketing professionals to adopt a scattergun approach to target customer selection. Choosing coverage over conversion, or market profile over penetration, will always end in tears, missed revenue targets and small commission checks.

Selling is not just a numbers game. Sure, if you don't make the calls and don't have the necessary coverage in the field, it is not possible to make your revenue numbers. On the other hand, if you are calling on the wrong people, or the right people but with the wrong offering or message, you will waste sales resource or burn valuable opportunities. Effective selling is about quality not quantity, profiling your target buyer, and assessing your offering from the customer's perspective. If you are getting positive responses from 10% of the targets you contact, you are wasting 90% of your time. Spend the time on the right customers, by selecting them well, and you will need to contact fewer customers to get better results.

Consider why sales transactions occur. A purchase is made when the buyer considers that the total cost expended is less than the total value received. The two easily identifiable aspects of this equation are 'total cost' and 'value received'.

The total cost is a combination of the product price and the cost of the implementation of the product to meet the needs of the buyer. Xerox and other copier vendors expressed their product cost, not as the capital expenditure of the equipment, but as the per-page cost for each copy. Buyers of enterprise software applications include the software license fee cost plus annual maintenance fees, hardware amortization and internal resource usage, to determine the total cost of ownership (TCO) of the software solution. Air travelers, when looking at low fares airlines, factor in flexibility and the potential extra travel time and costs if the airline does not fly into a major airport. Total cost is one side of the equation.

However, deals are not always won or lost on cost. Until value and pain exist in the mind of the buyer, any price is too high. Effective communication, or expression of value, is the oxygen that winning sales professionals breathe. Value is not just the list of product features and benefits matched to the buyer's stated needs. For every overt need stated by a buyer, there is pain and consequential impact if that need is not met, or the pain is not cured. Extending the buyer's vision, to enhance the potential gain that he envisions, is a function of true understanding of his business needs and personal and corporate goals. The vision should encompass the potential benefit to be delivered by the creative application of your product, your company, and the expertise of the salesperson. When you consider how you can align the total value you bring to the hidden, or unspoken, or even subconscious needs of the buyer, you can then begin to understand how you might express that value and create a gulf between you and your competition.

The best product does not always win. Think Apple versus IBM, or PowerPoint versus Harvard Graphics. Your product must meet the needs of the customers. But all customers value vendors in a multitude of ways. You have features they don't care about. Some things you do, they find irritating, but not terminally so. There are basic features you provide that are expected. You don't get any credit for those. Then there are the few specific needs that the customer cares about deeply. If you can satisfy those requirements with your complete solution, the customer sees real value and cares less about the competitor's feature-laden "über-product". Focus on the value – from the customer's perspective.

Choosing who *not* to do business with is sometimes easier than choosing those with whom you should engage. Where competitors are stronger than you are – move on. If customers are married to traditional practices and your offering promises advantage through discontinuous innovation – look elsewhere. If your product is leading edge, your customer must fit the profile of an early adopter.

Customers' demands are increasing and standards are high. As you redesign your efforts to make it as easy as possible for a customer to buy, you must consider the specific profile of that customer. Otherwise, you will fail to meet his exacting needs.

Value must be expressed, and value expression implies that you understand the position you want to occupy in the mind of the buyer. Positioning is not about you, your product or your company, but about the place in the customer's mind that you want to inhabit. If, from the broad expanse of the world's companies, you have selected your customer targets well, customers chosen to meet the inherent value of your product, and pruned by profile to meet the competitive advantage you bring, then your positioning should self-suggest. It will encompass an expression of value that sets you apart as the preferred supplier or customer partner. And this is where well-directed, strategic marketing travels side-by-side with effective selling. The determination of what specific value you can provide to a customer better than anyone else is the one silver bullet that is crucial to the sales role. Successful companies are not concerned about marketing activity to win marketing awards; they are focused on providing a compelling expression of value that helps them win sales awards.

In **Chapter 3: Select a Customer Value Proposition**, we offer some pointers to help you implement a framework to select the right customer every time. Coupled with your unique differentiated value, clearly understood and articulated, this consistent approach can be the catalyst for unparalleled revenue acceleration in your chosen market. You won't always get the deal – but you can rest assured that you will be in the right place, at the right time, with the right offering, more of the time.

Understand Buyer Need – Embrace the Buyer's Perspective

Take the time to stroll through your customer's mind and you will find the paths to success and failure signposted. Consider why he would buy your product, and mull over why he might not. The buyer might be an individual, a company or a committee, but the phases of the purchase process are generally the same. Understand that emotions change at the different phases of the buying cycle, as the customer moves from project initiation to the risk-laden final decision. And yes, it's a *buying* cycle – not a selling cycle.

Getting to understand the buyer's perspective is about listening, probing, questioning, and navigating through a layered corporation. In **Chapter 4: The Buyer's Perspective**, we provide some guidelines. We introduce the multiple buyers involved in each sale and segment the buying cycle into the four phases of Requirements, Evidence, Acquisition and Post-Sale, providing guidance on the different emotions and motivation at play in the buyer's mind, for each of the buyers. This gives you the opportunity to match your sales tactics to those needs, creating greater alignment of objectives.

Before you can change it, you have to get inside the buyer's mind. The deep listening skills and advanced questioning techniques covered in **Chapter 5: Discover, Develop & Control the Opportunity** help you to reveal the buyer's hidden motivations and true needs. Understanding the product feature requirements, service level expectations, and the other goals of the buyer's company, is crucial but doesn't suffice. Personal aspirations, fears and excitement live in the mind of the buyer and must be identified. Concerns for job security sometimes battle with the ambition of the corporate buyer. It used to always be safe to 'buy IBM'. Zero personal risk is generally good and sometimes the path of least resistance is the one with the signpost labeled 'Do Nothing'. Your job is to make it easy for the buyer to buy your product. Assuming you have targeted a company in your 'sweet spot', then, looking at it objectively, you should have a great shot at making the sale. But companies don't buy things – people buy things and you must understand the buyer's perspective. This is only possible if you anticipate behavior, watch for signals, empathize and look at things from the other side of the table. You must walk in your buyer's shoes.

In this new world, the professional salesperson – historically, the message carrier – is the value creator, the customer confidante, the trusted advisor and advocate. The equity value of the sales person has increased, as he owns the trust of the customer. Today's sales leaders balance the needs of the customers, which they truly understand, with the revenue and profitability of their own employer. Deep understanding of the metrics that drive both equips the shrewd sales professional with a differentiated opportunity to optimize return for all parties. Knowing what the customers want to buy, how they want to buy, what issues really matter to them, and what matters less, matched with knowledge of your true capability, allows the salesperson strike a true win-win bargain; notwithstanding the salesperson's inherent bias, which is that commission is what counts.

Customers rarely care about price alone. They care about value and return on investment. Successful sales professionals sell solutions and value. Price is only one factor. If the customer only cared about price, the salesforce would be redundant. The customers you want care about quality, dependability, ease of access, personalized service, customized solutions, company stability, and long-term relationships. Have you ever bought a product and thought, "That guy was really nice; he knew exactly what I wanted, wasn't too pushy and just let me make up my own mind"? Well, chances are 'that guy' knew exactly what he wanted, and guided you along his chosen path. You probably didn't even negotiate too hard at the end.

Qualify the Opportunity

The first organization that implemented the **SELECT SELLING** model was a Fortune 500 technology company. We had worked with that company for a period of time on sales, marketing and strategic issues. The company was doing well in a young, growing market, and running at about a 30% annual growth rate. However, Carol, the Vice President of Sales, wasn't satisfied.

The scenario was an interesting one. The market was moving quickly, prospects were plentiful, and an opportunity existed to accelerate revenue growth dramatically, and to attain a dominant market position. But competitors were looming, the ratio of prospect to sales conversion wasn't great, and the rate of implementation of the company's solution by its customers was slower than desired - resulting in revenue per customer being less than was anticipated.

Our challenge: design a sales process and help Carol implement it!

Carol was in the fortunate position of leading an enthusiastic sales team in a dynamic market, with more opportunities than they knew what to do with. However, that was part of the problem; they didn't know what to do with all of them. They were not qualifying their opportunities and were chasing deals that they could never win - or deals that were so competitive they weren't worth winning at the price. The second hitch was that, because they were flush with opportunities, they sold using what we would call the 'fly by' approach - a low-altitude pass over many customers, occasionally parachuting in to try to close a deal. They got the deals but, because they hadn't spent time with the customers helping them to understand the operational issues and inherent behavioral changes required for a successful implementation, the customers made slow progress, and the transaction-related fees were slow in coming. The third major difficulty was that the other supporting departments in the company - marketing, operations and product development - were running hither and thither, responding to an expansive range of issues from a diverse selection of customers, and serving nobody well.

Do you recognize this scenario? It's far too common – but it's a set of problems that can be solved easily with a disciplined approach to qualification and the attendant behavioral changes. Behavior change is about you, your company and your customers. It's how you act, how your colleagues act, and how your customers act. With you and your colleagues, the issues are fairly simple, once you accept the basic tenets put forward in this book. Assuming you are targeting the right customer, with the right offering, a rigorous qualification system is the most important process to implement. When it's pervasive in your company, it drives uncommonly productive behavior. In **Chapter 6: Do**

You Qualify to Sell?, we ask the question, "Why work on unqualified opportunities when you could be making money?" and we provide the **SELECT SELLING 4M Qualification Model** to help you pick the winning prospects.

You need to chase the right deals – deals that you have a great chance of winning. When you are operating in this mode, your colleagues are fully aligned with you, with a complete understanding of their purpose. When that happens, the company moves as a single effective unit, energy is focused on the right activity, sales efficiency levels rise, and revenue grows.

Benefits to the customer are only delivered when the technology is adopted. Only with usage comes value, and that truism is at the heart of the need to focus on implementation issues, as part of the qualification process. A customer who has received value is a happy customer, and when revenue is in any way related to usage, you must be doubly focused on helping the customer through the transformation that accompanies change.

And what about Carol?

In the first full quarter after they implemented **SELECT SELLING**, Carol's team achieved 200% of their revenue goal. It's nice to see it work!

Plan & Manage the Pipeline

We have designed the SELECT SELLING sales process to incorporate stages in the pipeline that reflect the customer's buying cycle. It seems more logical to us to link the selling cycle to the customer's buying cycle than to use other measures that sometimes seem arbitrary. If you take this approach, the SELECT SELLING activity that you have to plan becomes self-apparent.

Maintaining a strong pipeline, with enough qualified opportunities at each phase in the pipeline, is the only way to avoid the quarter-end crunch that often results in unnecessary discounting just to make your quarter's number. **Chapter 7: The SELECT SELLING Pipeline Management System** shows you how to link precise qualification with your pipeline management system, and build credible sales forecasts – forecasts everyone can believe in – to help you avoid those revenue troughs.

Execute the Sale

The SELECT SELLING process recognizes that selling a complex solution to a large corporation is a multi-layered, multi-event journey. **Chapter 8: Implement SELECT SELLING: Sales Action Planning** includes the tools you need to assess your position in a sale, determine the next optimum destination, and develop a map to get you there. At each juncture, you need to view things from the customer's perspective. What is to the forefront of his mind right now? Is it risk, features, value, timing, price, or a combination of all of these? Understanding what the customer wants to achieve, and delivering to those requirements, opens the door for you to make progress towards your own goals.

We hope that the steps outlined here will help you sell the right solution, to the right customers, through good targeting and rigorous qualification. By following the right steps, you should feel more confident about becoming your customer's partner, and gain layered access throughout the customer's organization – making sure that you are touching all the influencers of a sale.

Negotiate & Close

Chapter 9: The Continuous Art of Complete Negotiation ensures you maximize the return on your efforts, as you become a Complete Negotiator – not just a tactician, but also a strategist. You understand the how, where and when of closing the sale. Concerned with substance more than style, you can perfect the art of crafting value-creating agreements, and control the ground rules to create a more favorable environment.

HOW TO USE SELECT SELLING

As you join us in our journey down the path of SELECT SELLING, we hope you will benefit from the principles we have outlined. We have designed the process to be practical and pragmatic. It has helped good sales professionals and sales managers to become superior performers, and has been the catalyst for growth to help good CEOs build great companies. We've seen dramatic business transformation. We recommend that you treat this book as a resource, your constant companion, one you can turn to for advice and guidance as you navigate each turn in the road. Each major chapter in the book is accompanied by a worksheet, which you should treat as a map to determine your current location and way forward.

The worksheets have been crafted to guide your thoughts and to let you self-monitor, and to provoke with tough questions for you to ask yourself, before you are stumped by someone else. The tools and models that underpin **SELECT SELLING** have been road-tested, tuned and upgraded, to maximize sales effectiveness in this evolved economy. Complementary models and softcopy material are available on www.selectselling.com, for you to download and use. Use the worksheets and tools as often as you can, until the signposts therein become part of your own mental atlas that guides you to your destination.

Apply the book to meet your needs. **Chapter 2: How to be a Sales Specialist** is for anyone who wants to know what it takes to be a superior sales performer. It helps you to evaluate yourself and to develop your own personal improvement plan to excel in a value-driven career. The following chapter, **Chapter 3: Select a Customer Value Proposition**, is included to help you to state your unique value to your carefully selected customers. It's more strategic than tactical, and you should revisit it as you develop your higher-level plans, ensuring that the resultant output is implemented in everything you do. **Chapters 4** through **9** are concerned with the detail of the selling process. Every day, you need to think about your customer; qualify, question, manage, plan, and then execute and negotiate. This is the segment of the process where sales management and sales professionals will likely return to most frequently.

Bon voyage. Good luck and good **SELECT SELLING**.

CHAPTER 2

How to Become a Sales Specialist

The essence of value delivered by a sales person to his or her customer is a combination of the strategic value described in the last chapter, the sales process addressed later in the book and the specific value delivered by the individual sales professional. Whatever you think about anything else, you must take personal responsibility for the last of these. This chapter is about you – the sales professional. No escape, no excuses, nobody else to blame – the aspects of your behavior outlined in this chapter are under your control – it's up to you. If you left your company today, how much would your customers miss you? If it's 'not much', you have some work to do. If it's 'a lot', then keep doing what you are doing, and do more of it.

High-performance sales professionals tend to be more in tune with the shifting needs of their customers than their less successful counterparts. They engage in self-assessment and continuous learning. High-performers have deep industry knowledge that is applicable to their customer's business. They act as customer advocates and are viewed by the customer as trusted advisors. They have presentation, negotiation, and communication skills that are continuously honed and refined. High-performers are ambitious, motivated, confident – but not arrogant – and have strong business and analytical skills. They understand the principles of value selling. It's a tough proposition, and you don't get to be a high-performer without consistent application. Winning sales professionals need to be, at once, the performer, conductor, diplomat, negotiator, confidante, expert, and partner. This can only be achieved by hard work and focus in a specific niche. We call these focused high-performers *Sales Specialists*.

There are two axes on which success revolves for companies today – expertise and focus – and selling professionals today need to formulate their own business strategies in these terms. If the product or service you are selling has horizontal appeal, and has potential application across a whole range of different industries, please consider the benefits of adopting a vertical strategy, picking a sector you have some knowledge in, and becoming more expert than your customers in the application of your type of solution to their industry. Succeed in that sector and then look for the next closely aligned sector to dominate.

A financial software solution has, on the surface, broad horizontal application, but the application of a financial software package in the telecommunications industry varies greatly from its use in the hospitality sector. Different metrics apply in the two industries. Manufacturing software solutions differ as to their implementation in electronics and pharmaceutical sectors, the latter being focused largely on quality and compliance while the former is focused on efficiencies and cost reduction. It is much easier to discuss payroll issues with one hotel group when you have the experience of implementation with another. Reference selling, which we will discuss later, is also greatly accelerated by taking a vertical or niche approach. Your customers are far more likely to talk to each other if they are in the same business.

Concerns about limiting the opportunities you can pursue, or not having enough prospects to target, will logically come to the surface as you consider where you should focus. Human nature will interfere with the science of selling and you may naturally be inclined to try the smorgasbord approach, having a little taste of each sector rather than just going for the steak. For now, let's try to leave those concerns aside, and by the end of this chapter, we hope you will understand why we recommend this approach – the steak is more filling!

KNOW YOURSELF – THE SELECT SELLING SALES QUADRANT PROFILER

Figure 2, the **SELECT SELLING** Sales Quadrant Profiler, shows four different profiles of sales person, each with varying degrees of product expertise, industry specialization and consequent levels of success. The X-axis represents the degree of industry focus, and the Y-axis represents the level of knowledge in that industry.

FIGURE 2: THE SELECT SELLING SALES QUADRANT PROFILER

	Generalist	Specialist
	Generalist Low efficiency Makes quota - just! ***Could do better***	High hit rate Customer confidante Extremely focused ***Winner***
	Wishful Thinker	**Lazy Gambler**
	Big forecast All deals @ 90% No sales ***Fired frequently***	Lives off existing accounts and depends on bluebirds ***Parasite***

Depth of Product Expertise (vertical axis) · Industry Focus (horizontal axis)

In the first quadrant on bottom-left is the guy we term the **Wishful Thinker**, and we all know this guy. We worked with him, or hired him (we know we've done both). He is exuberant and fun, popular with the other departments, spends a lot of time cultivating relationships at the wrong level in his own company and the customer's organization. The Wishful Thinker will have a big pipeline and all of the deals are due to close 'real soon'. His problem – and it's his manager's predicament too – is that because he flits from sector to sector, he has little knowledge about any industry, he can't add value to the buyer, and he never quite understands the challenges his customers face. The consequence of this is he rarely closes any meaningful deals and gets fired frequently. The problem for the company, of course, is not just that it has wasted investment in training and salary, but the sales opportunities that were missed represent revenue lost forever – probably gone to a competitor, making them stronger.

Moving along the X-axis we have the **Lazy Gambler** who has probably worked in the same company, or certainly sold to the same industry for a long time. Consequently, he knows the sector well, but is too lazy to research how emerging trends impact his customers or to develop creative applications of the company's products to help his customers. This sales person is adept at identifying deals that are going to happen just because of his company's position in a market or his company's relationship with a particular company. He understands internal politics well and focuses a lot of his resources figuring out how he can claim the sale rather than generating his own deals. This activity was once described to us by an ex-IBM sales person as 'chasing the blue-money'. IBM was going to get the deal anyway and the only question was who was going to get the credit, and commission, for the deal. The Lazy Gambler is just a parasite and doesn't add any value to either his employer or his customers, and steals value from his colleagues.

In the upper left quadrant of the Sales Quadrant Profiler is the **Generalist**. Typically, the Generalist is very bright, but somewhat ill-disciplined and lacking in focus. Applying his intellect, he is able to think on his feet, and achieve a modicum of competence in many industries. He usually barely makes quota. But because there is no hub at the center of his activity, and because he believes that he knows just about enough to get by, he underachieves, and surrenders his innate advantage, and his edge, to his more disciplined colleagues and competitors. Believing that he has the ability to sell anything to anyone, the Generalist's credibility suffers and he fails to develop deep sustainable relationships with customers, as he flutters from industry to industry.

The most successful salesperson we ever met lives and works in a small city in upstate New York. Matt has four very large customers whose headquarters are based nearby. Over the 15 or so years we've known Matt, he has had three different employers, all in technology, but he has always retained the same four major customers. The companies are in similar sectors, and Matt is considered locally to be an expert in that industry. Every year, Matt worked with his customers to develop their vision for the coming year and they looked to him for guidance and advice. For the few years that we had direct business contact with Matt, he consistently achieved more than twice his annual quota and was always one of the top three performing sales people in whichever company he worked.

Matt is a **Sales Specialist**. His laser-like focus on the business he knows helps him identify target opportunities that he can win. Because of that level of focus and restraint, he avoids the chaos of the numbers game and he can take the time to become a 'thought leader' in the issues that his customers worry about. He makes connections with customers rather than contacts. In our experience, his sales hit rate was outstanding. His forecasts were impeccably accurate. His customers viewed him as their 'go-to' guy to help them deliver on their business initiatives. He successfully transcended the relationship barrier to become a partner, rather than being perceived just as a vendor.

FIRST STEPS TO BECOMING A SALES SPECIALIST

It has never been so important to get close to your customer. Buyers have big problems that they want solved and they want to be able to trust someone to help them. Now, we know that we continue to emphasize this point, but unless you select one area to specialize in, your chance of success is severely reduced.

Later in this chapter, we set out the 20 specific detailed elements that you should evaluate in yourself so that you can self-assess and see whether you make the grade. For now, let's look at *four key things* you should look at to raise your game:

1. **Become a recognized 'thought leader' in your customer's industry**: The first step you have to take is to immerse yourself in the business. Read the trade publications. Attend seminars and conferences. Review what the industry analysts are saying. Talk to your customers about the key challenges they face over the coming years. Look to the whitepapers offered by your competitors. Read the SEC filings of the public companies in the sector. Use the Internet to research what opinion-makers are saying. Get to understand the dynamics of the sector, and develop profiles of the key industry influencers. Find out the names of the key trade or professional associations, and join the local chapter. Talk to other sales professionals who sell non-competing products to the same sector. Listen and learn. Now you're qualified to play.

   Research upcoming events and offer yourself as a speaker. Write a short opinion piece on what you have gleaned as the main challenges your customers face and get it published in a trade journal. If you don't have writing skills, get someone to help you with the writing. Use the opinion piece as a basis for a customer survey. Talk to the 10 largest players in the sector and ask them to participate in a thought leader's survey, soliciting their valuable opinions on your hypothesis. Offer them a copy of the survey analysis in return for their opinion. Get the results of the survey published. Now, when customers have problems or issues, they will be more inclined to think about you than your competitor. Unless you're superhuman, you can only do this in one industry at a time, but don't you think that if you've achieved thought leadership in your chosen industry you can achieve your goals? You will certainly get more opportunities at the right level in your prospective accounts.

2. **Gain 'trusted advisor' status:** Trust is not easily won. It starts with integrity. It starts with you being able to say to yourself honestly that the product or service offering that you represent can, when applied appropriately, deliver real value to the customer. If you don't believe this, then you will not be able to convince the customers that it is true. Nor should you try. Integrity is a core business asset. Never undertake to sell products that you believe don't deliver value to the customer. It's not right and it will come back to haunt you.
   To become an advisor you must be competent, and you must have knowledge that is more extensive in some areas than that of your customer. Sometimes, the customer is too busy trying to deal with problems internal to his company to review everything going on around him. That's your job. Combining expertise, integrity and a true desire to help your customer produces surprising results and sometimes uncommon actions. You will find yourself calling the customer with recently acquired information that is of value to him, without looking for anything in return. If the implementation of your product is not going well, you will find the customer calling you to point it out before it becomes a big issue. You are both on the same side and you find yourself, in partnership with your customer, using the word 'we' a lot, rather than 'I' or 'you'.

3. **Be a complete communicator:** Listen, question, listen again, then speak, write and present. Listening skills, while frequently referenced, are rarely exercised well. You cannot learn if you don't listen; a good listener will beat a fast talker anytime. Later in this book, we discuss the **SELECT SELLING** Progressive Questioning Control Model, a method for you to use to ask increasingly powerful questions. You have two ears and one mouth; use them in that proportion. Inexperienced sales people are often so interested in what they themselves have to say next that they don't listen well. Highly developed listening and questioning skills will speed your understanding and help you to develop the right solution for the customer at the first attempt.
   Once you have something valuable to say, you must consider how you present it. In a world increasingly dominated by email and voice-mail, you must pay due attention to how you communicate in these mediums. Sloppiness and casual correspondence is somehow

deemed acceptable when communicating by email, but it says a lot to your customer about how much (or how little) you care, if you don't take the time to craft your emails carefully, checking grammar and spelling, and using appropriate etiquette. As your customers' use of voicemail has almost certainly become more prevalent, you should be prepared to leave a good voice-mail message. No 'emming and aahhing'. Before making the call, think about what you want to say if the customer picks up, and what you want to say if he doesn't. As you write proposals, or script presentations, consider that the document or presentation you are submitting may be received by other influential people, not just the person you have been speaking with. Each document should be complete in itself, so that you are not relying on previous communication with one individual to be passed on to others. If you are not good at writing proposals, seek the help of a colleague or friend. Always use the spell-checker and grammar-checker in your word-processor.

Communication is at the heart of business. It's a skill to be learned, practiced and honed. In every sales situation, at all times, either you are making progress or sliding backwards – things never stay the same. Unless your communication, spoken or written, will advance the sale, then keep it to yourself.

4. **Engage in continuous self-improvement and education:** You have to work hard to stay on top of your game. Commenting recently on the developments in modern business, Peter Drucker said,

   > "There has been a revolution in the way that work is performed within most organizations, but the relationship between organizations themselves is changing just as fast, and this is the sales revolution".

   As mentioned earlier in this chapter, the sales role is increasingly about value *creation*, rather than value *communication*. Today's sales professional must make a continuous effort to remain expert, so that he can be that value creator. Whoever can help the fastest, with the most expertise, makes the difference. That calls for continuous rapid learning. You must learn not to rely on being the best in the past. Every day, you must strive to keep your position as your customer's trusted advisor. That means learning faster than the customer (and the competition) and being expert in his processes.

So, if you are a Sales Specialist, you are recognized as an expert in one industry. You have worked hard on your communications skills. Your customer views you as his business partner, not just another vendor and you persist with your self-education to retain your position at the top of the pile. What does it all get you?

Niche market penetration

In the previous chapter, we set out some guidelines for target customer selection. If you followed those guidelines, you will have developed a Customer Value Proposition that connects with your target market, setting out your competitive advantage. It makes sense then, to focus on that niche market. If you deliver well for one customer in a sector, it is easier to replicate that success with another customer within the same sector, than to find a new customer in a different sector. Selling to airlines today, pharmaceuticals tomorrow and telecommunications next week means that you have to re-establish your credentials every time. Customers look to companies that they can relate to when looking for an example of a successful implementation of your product. Buyers in competing companies in the same sector will frequently talk to each other about their problems. Your customer can sometimes be your best advocate and your most fruitful source of opportunities. As you begin to gather a number of customers in one sector, you can attain a defendable position that will be hard for the competition to take away from you.

Contacts, connections and referral opportunities

Being perceived as a 'thought leader' will get you visibility in the sector. It's amazing how everyone seems to know everything about everyone in their industry – at least locally. Your fame will spread, and you will have the opportunity to turn this increased number of contacts into true business connections and, ultimately, into customers.

Most importantly, however, if you have a track record of delivering real value to your customer, because you are the 'trusted advisor' who is expert and continuously stays ahead in the knowledge game, your customers will be comfortable passing on referral opportunities to you – if you ask. When you perform well for the new customer, it reflects well on the customer who referred you. Similarly, when your satisfied customer moves on to a new job, he is likely to do so within the industry. Rarely do senior executives move to entirely new sectors. When they get established in their new company, you are immediately presented with a potential new opportunity.

Knowledge & Power

If you are a Sales Specialist, you probably know the organizational hierarchy of each of the target customers in the industry in which you specialize. You know the influencers in the business. You're aware when industry associations are making recommendations to their members to implement a new technology solution to deal with an upcoming regulatory matter. You're probably helping the standards committee draft the recommendations. You have the inside track, and you're a jump ahead of the competition. As you meet with industry players at social events, you will learn different nuggets of information that you would never hear about in a more formal setting. Knitting together all the strands of knowledge and tidbits or data that you gather creates a much more informative picture of the industry in general, and the individual companies in particular. Knowledge is power, but it takes time and investment to get.

The Evolution of a Sales Specialist

Sales Specialists are professional about their crafts. They sharpen their skills constantly and engage in continuous self-appraisal and education. None of this is easily achieved, nor are there salespeople gratuitously ordained at birth with all the selling skills they will ever need. Getting to this point is a series of steps. Most sales professionals begin by selling product features, and then progress to selling against competition in the market. As their business skills become more honed, the next stage of evolution is selling complex solutions to meet stated business needs. Only a few graduate to become true creators of value. Only the best become Sales Specialists. **Figure 3** shows how they evolve.

FIGURE 3: HOW A SALES SPECIALIST EVOLVES

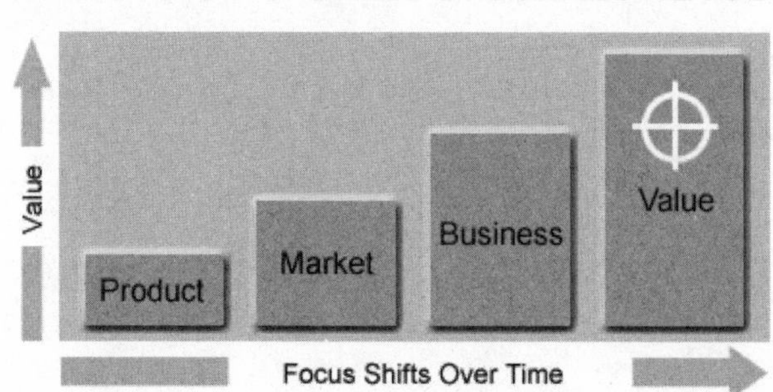

ARE YOU A SALES SPECIALIST?

When two people want to do business together, the details of the deal won't hold them apart. Getting your customer into that frame of mind happens only when you have done your homework and shown yourself to be a true value creator. If you are selling to professionals, you must be a professional. If you are selling to C-level executives, you must act like one – you must create value for your customer.

We have identified 20 distinctive factors (see **Figure 4**) that, when put together, seem to represent what is best about the best.

FIGURE 4: THE SELECT SELLING SALES SPECIALIST MONITOR

	VALUE SELLING		CUSTOMER PERSPECTIVE		INDUSTRY KNOWLEDGE		PERSONAL ATTRIBUTES
1	Ability to express value clearly	9	Be a trusted advisor	13	Know industry influencers	16	Listening and questioning
2	Understand why you win deals	10	Engage comfortably at the most senior level	14	Join industry networking groups	17	Effective communication and presentation skills
3	Ask for referrals (not a testimonial)	11	Act as a customer advocate	15	Strength of personal Rolodex	18	Motivated and confident
4	Follow a defined sales process	12	Understand the customer's business			19	Negotiation skills
5	Ask why you lost the deal					20	Business and analytical skills
6	Pursue only well-qualified leads						
7	Be able to differentiate against each major competitor						
8	Have a plan to address most common objections						

These factors encompass *industry knowledge* for the chosen sector, proficiency in *value selling* skills, incorporating product knowledge and application of the product to the customer's business problem, understanding the *customer perspective*, and above all, *personal attributes* of the sales professional. Attention to the principles outlined here will help – whether you are evaluating your own performance, interviewing candidates to hire or helping a fellow sales person develop a self-improvement plan.

It's up to you to take it from here. We know that 20 factors are a lot to go through, but stick with it – it will be worth it! Review these attributes and consider how well they describe your competencies or attitude. Then score yourself. Honesty counts and pays off. The exercise should help you to identify any areas of weakness in your sales proficiency and will provide a framework for a self-improvement plan. For sales management, review these points for new hires and decide for yourself what score they need for a pass grade.

Value Selling

Until value (and pain) exists in the mind of a customer, any price is too high. Therefore, you must:

1. **Be able to express value clearly:** You need to be able to articulate clearly the value of your complete product or service offering in terms the customer understands and values. "I have a pill that cures your headache." This assumes you understand the cause of the headache, and that your solution is the morphine to cure the pain. Sometimes, it is useful to ask your existing customers to explain to you why they bought your product. Or ask them what they would tell their counterparts in other companies if asked about your offering. Then craft your own message, test and refine it, and keep it up-to-date.

2. **Understand why you win deals:** People rarely buy from people they don't like, but the reasons customers buy are many and varied. To repeat success, it is important to understand the reason for your success. Rigorous analysis of sales wins helps you to identify those elements of your offering that take the cover off your customer's signing pen. What were the 'hot buttons' the customer cared about? Was price a factor? What was your competitive advantage? Did the customer buy because of product features, your company's market position, or just your outstanding selling skills? This analysis helps

you to play to your strengths and to refine the profile of your ideal opportunity. It guides you to further opportunities within existing accounts. It helps you win more often.

3. **Ask for referrals (not a testimonial):** Marketing departments in technology companies spend a lot of time and effort looking for 'testimonials' from existing customers to put on the website, in order to attract more prospects. And we all know such testimonials are hard to get. In a Fortune 100 company, it is often as difficult to navigate the layers of sign-off and authorization for a public statement as it was to get budget approval for the original deal. You should spend *your* time getting verbal referrals. A recommendation from an industry peer will do a lot to enhance your credibility and open doors faster than you could yourself. It will certainly be quicker than waiting for the testimonial on the website to generate quality leads. Pick your target account and then ask your existing customer if they know anyone in that company. Customers who have successful implementations of technology solutions like to recount their successes. It reflects well on them, and can accelerate your sales cycle dramatically. Now, ask yourself: "When did I last ask for a referral from one of my existing customers?".

4. **Follow a defined sales process:** Whether it's the SELECT SELLING methodology, or something else, you must have a plan, with a start, a middle and an end. To reach your revenue goal consistently, you must have many prospects at different stages in the sales pipeline at all times. You need to understand what stage of the buying cycle the customer is at, before you develop a plan to progress through the selling cycle. Customer selection, opportunity qualification, proposal, presentation, short-list, negotiation and contracts are all stages that typically take time, and each stage will deliver its own challenges and casualties. Think about it, make your assumptions, have a plan, test the assumptions and recalibrate, and then execute to the plan.

5. **Ask why you lost the deal:** "But they'll never tell me the truth!". Well, our evidence suggests that, if you have been fair and honest with your potential customers, and have made a *bona fide* effort to address the requirements of the sale, you will be told the reason why you didn't get the deal. If you have selected the customer well, and were truly qualified to win, then somewhere along the line you were outperformed by your competition. It's better to know the reason

than to skulk away with your tail between your legs. There will be more opportunities in that account, and learning from your mistakes will prepare you better for the next go-around. You will also learn about your competitors and the customer's view of their strengths over yours. Knowledge about your adversary will equip you with additional intelligence for other competitive situations. Overcome the natural inclination to wallow in the disappointment and don't allow yourself to sink to denigrating the customer for making the wrong decision. Make the call and learn from the experience.

6. **Pursue only well-qualified leads:** Your time is limited. In a complex selling situation, you need to spend considerable time orchestrating resources, developing relationships, gaining access at multiple layers in an organization, examining how your solution can be applied best to the customer's business, determining how you can add value best, testing your hypothesis and refining and reworking the solution you are creating with the customer. There are only so many opportunities you can pursue properly at the same time. Qualify hard. Examine budgets, buying process, buyer access, project timeframe and decision-making process, and then decide whether you think you can win the deal and if it's worth winning. Pick potential winners early and sort out the wheat from the chaff. Use the **SELECT SELLING 4M Qualification Worksheet** that you will find in **Figure 26** to determine whether the prospect is worth pursuing. Be ruthless in prioritizing where you spend your time. You must zone in on the good prospects and leave less attractive opportunities aside. Select customers and opportunities well, and then decide to do what it takes to win those deals.

7. **Be able to differentiate against each major competitor:** We estimate that more than half of sales people underestimate their competition – or don't research them adequately. You know who your major competitors are likely to be in most situations. Can you articulate clearly why the customer should buy from you rather than the bigger, established player? What advantages do you have over the new market entrant with the exciting new technology? What's the customer's perspective of the strengths of each of these competitors? If your company is smaller than that of your adversary, then perhaps you are more agile, flexible or responsive. If your competitor is the new kid on the block, then maybe you are the stable, safe, proven industry standard. Undoubtedly, there will be strengths and

weaknesses for each player. You must know these and be prepared to position appropriately, depending on which competitors you are up against in a particular account. Never underestimate the competitor or belittle them to your customer. Be clear about how to express your value in the context of the competitive situation.

8. **Have a plan to address most common objections:** Objections arise when a customer has concerns about your company or product, as they relate to the problem the customer is trying to solve. Objections are not spurious obstacles put in your way to test you. Objections should be addressed, not overcome. Recognize that there is a possibility that some prospects won't raise all their objections, and you should use the questioning techniques, outlined later in the book, to uncover hidden concerns.
   Consider the customer's perspective. If your price is higher than expected, or greater than your competitor's, then the customer has a real problem to deal with if he proceeds with purchasing your product. You must be prepared to help him address that problem, if you are to win the deal. Product feature concerns can often be addressed by understanding what benefit the customer is looking to achieve or what problem he is trying to solve. Consider how your company can overcome a deficit in the product by adding a service offering. That will suffice in some instances. At least, it shows that you understand the issue and are prepared to address it. Value selling will overcome minor price objections. "Yes, I agree with you that we are not the cheapest and here are the reasons why…" Embrace the buyer's perspective and work with him to come up with a solution that addresses his concerns. Objections are concerns to be addressed, not obstacles to be overcome. Be aware of the most common concerns, and be ready to help.

Customer Perspective

To change the customer's mind, you first have to get inside it. Therefore, you must:

9. **Be a trusted advisor:** We referenced this point earlier in the chapter, but it's important and you need to constantly review your 'trusted advisor' status. It is not enough anymore to have an innovative product, superlative customer service, or a cost-effective solution. The bar has been raised dramatically and each of these items becomes a culling factor, rather than a differentiator. Your customers

are bombarded every day by multiple vendors, possibly with solutions that are better, cheaper or faster. The customer is looking, however, not for a vendor, but for a partner, someone he can trust, can share the pain with, is knowledgeable and is in the relationship for the long term. In short, he is looking for someone he can trust to help him make the right decision for his business. He will treat his 'trusted advisor' almost as a part of his team, sharing concerns and uncertainties that will never be discussed with vendors. As a trusted advisor, you can help shape strategy, construct terms of reference for upcoming projects, and get to understand the real issues that customers care about. Trust is not transferable. You cannot be handed an account from a colleague and immediately assume the role of trusted advisor. It's a rare and valuable position, and you need to build it, one truth at a time.

10. **Engage comfortably at the most senior level:** If you want to sell to executives, you have to act like one, read the same business and trade publications, attend the same conferences, and be professional in everything that you do. More importantly, however, to be comfortable as you interact with very senior executives in large corporations, you must believe in yourself and your ability to add real value to their situation. If you fundamentally believe that you can help, and that belief is not based on blind faith or groundless assumptions, then you have a right to be at the table – and you know it. With knowledge and hard work come experience, confidence (not arrogance), and mutual respect, and that's the basis for a really strategic partnership with your customer.

11. **Act as a customer advocate:** It may require a change of mindset from the traditional view, but a Sales Specialist acts as a campaigner to make sure his customer succeeds, having built internal relationships to expedite getting things done. Increasingly, successful organizations are creating cultures throughout their companies that inculcate a customer-centric perspective. At the front-line, customers expect you to be the primary contact and to be their advocate, promoting their interests, and sponsoring activities to optimize the successful application of your offering in their organization. Customer advocacy deepens relationships, and relegates price considerations to second or third place. As an advocate, you will always be proactive, anticipating needs, maintaining frequent

contact with your customer, and acting as a bridge to your colleagues who participate in issue resolution.

12. **Understand the customer's business:** What are the key metrics your customer uses to measure success? What's the typical cost of customer acquisition in his industry? What are the growth challenges in the sector? Are there new disruptive technologies being introduced that present opportunities? What external factors impact on growth; regulatory, economic, demographic or social? What role does the Internet play in supply chain efficiencies or introduction of new competitors? In the hotel sector, it's all about occupancy rates. For low-cost airlines, the strategic business imperative is operational efficiency. As online travel companies address the corporate sector, the return is directly linked to levels of adoption of their online booking tools. The customer acquisition cost for a typical wireless telecommunication company is about $400. A major challenge for healthcare giants is FDA regulatory compliance. How well do you understand the business drivers for your chosen niche? How does your product or solution solve the customer's pain?

Industry Knowledge

Don't be dependent just on what you know about your product or your customer. The state of their industry is the context for their decisions. Therefore, you must:

13. **Know industry influencers:** In the CRM business, companies read the newsletters published by Bob Thompson of CRMGuru. Looking for trends in Search Engines, consult Danny Sullivan at SearchEngineWatch. Beyond these 'boutique influencers', each sector is covered by analysts from organizations such as Forrester Research, Jupiter Research, IDC, or Gartner Group. Buyers look to these influencers to help them in the early stages of their purchasing decisions. You need to know who the influencers are for your specific sector, and understand their perspective on trends in your target industry. You must make sure they are briefed on your offering. Hopefully, you will find one that supports your perspective. If not, you need to be prepared when your potential customer asks you about the influencer's viewpoint.

14. **Join industry networking groups:** The chances are your customers are actively involved in the local association for their industry. So too are your competitors. Generally it's a place to learn and network, develop co-operative relationships with complementary vendors and relationships with potential customers, in an informal setting. The more progressive associations host dinners, functions and seminars, bringing in experts from all fields to help you gain more perspective on your customer's business. You could get involved in the industry awards selection committee, which might recognize the best company in a specific part of your business. Where else would you get the opportunity to get such insight into the best players? Participate in special interest group meetings or networking dinner meetings, and other high visibility events, and you have a powerful competitive resource. The more you put into these types of associations, the more you get out.

15. **Strength of personal Rolodex:** A Sales Specialist has a wealth of personal industry contacts. These contacts have been cultivated over time, built through effective networking and strengthened through an experience of trust and mutual respect. Every relationship matters, and treating customers, competitors or colleagues with respect and integrity helps build your list of precious contacts. When you come across some valuable information, take some time to consider who in your contact base might value it. Pass it on and it's likely they will reciprocate. A broad contact base enhances your ability to gain access to companies or individuals you don't know, or gather information on a prospect or competitor.

Personal Attributes

In the end, it all comes down to the individual sales professional. People buy from people they like. People buy from professionals. Most of all, they buy from people they can trust. The following five attributes are fundamental to your success:

16. **Listening and questioning:** While most sales people have been trained to listen well, few have practiced deep listening skills and questioning methods. Sales Specialists allow the customer to talk, and really listen to what the customer has to say rather than thinking about what to say next. They keep control of the conversation flow by having a structured questioning technique that is only fluid in its adapting to the scenario at hand. Effective selling involves

preparation, and Sales Specialists will have specific objectives documented for every meeting, and a set of questions designed to lead the customer to present the information required or come up with thoughts aligned to the seller's goals.

17. **Effective communication and presentation skills:** There is an overwhelming correlation between strong, powerful and evocative communication and credibility, respect and success. A Sales Specialist is an effective messenger whose verbal communications, presentations and proposals are informative, inclusive, inviting of comment, context-sensitive, substantive, and powerful. They confer respect and leadership attributes on the source. Sales Specialists work to hone their communication skills – both written and verbal. They communicate concepts confidently and with impact, are remembered and acknowledged for their ideas, and are acclaimed as intelligent provocative leaders.

18. **Motivated and confident:** People lacking in motivation tend to avoid results-related chores because they tend to doubt their ability and believe that success is dependent on 'who you know' or on other factors outside of their control. They work with little drive or enthusiasm, because they don't see the relationship between effort and results. Sales Specialists are highly motivated, take on challenges and are driven to be in charge of whatever sales situation they find themselves in, taking ownership and responsibility for their sales quota. They believe in their ability to take control over their own destiny and success. You notice when a successful sales person enters the room: they have poise and presence and a confidence based on self-belief and lots of preparation. Confidence begets confidence and the Sales Specialist induces calm in the mind of the buyer through his composure and firm but flexible determination to get the job done.

19. **Negotiation skills:** While mediocre sales people can often close deals, they frequently leave money on the table and allow profit margins to be eroded through ineffective negotiation. Selling and buying are two sides of the same coin, and successful negotiation requires that you understand the other party's stated and unstated needs, their point of view and their 'walk-away' position. Great sales professionals will have practiced negotiation techniques, understand the structures of strategy and counter-strategy, how to satisfy needs by uncovering them and when to walk away. Negotiation requires

clarification of assumptions – yours and theirs, and the ability to separate real interests from adopted positions. Remember as you sell, negotiation is often about negotiation of information. Sales Specialists become the Complete Negotiators described in **Chapter 9**.

20. **Business and analytical skills:** If you are selling to businesses, you have to understand how business works. When customers look for return on investment analysis for the total cost of implementing your product, you need to understand the elements of their business that contribute to their costs. There are as many reasons why people buy products as there are products, but it nearly always comes down to financial metrics. You need to understand the rules by which this game is played. Some companies are looking to increase revenue, others seek cost-reduction and short-term profits, while many have specific measures of ROI performance. You must have the ability to understand and analyze both the macro-economic factors that impact your customer's industry, and the micro-economic elements that are the guide-rails for his specific investment in your product or service. You should question yourself as to how conversant you are with general business issues. Do you read *BusinessWeek, Fortune, Forbes*, the *Wall Street Journal, Financial Times,* and your local business paper? How comfortable are you with basic financial analysis? Now, you don't need to know the minutiae of GAAP, Sarbanes-Oxley, or Higgs, but you should know what they mean and their impact on your customer. If you are selling to public companies, you should be able to read SEC filings and standard financial statements. To be a great salesperson, to be a Sales Specialist, you first need to be a businessperson.

If you want to use the **SELECT SELLING** Sales Specialist Monitor Worksheet to evaluate yourself, or a potential new hire, a softcopy of the template is available at www.selectselling.com for you to download.

THE VALUE JUST MIGHT BE YOU

At certain stages in the maturity of a market, many of the products just blend together with no clear differentiation that the customer really cares about from a pure product features perspective. It is then up to you to demonstrate your value. Show the customer how your skill, expertise and experience can differentiate the application of your offering from that of your competitor.

For the traditional sales person, this is a foreign concept, something not to be undertaken under any circumstances and so he resorts to discounting and a price war to try to win the business. The Sales Specialist welcomes this paradigm. He is well-equipped to play and will often deliver extraordinary value to his customer. The customer gets a consultant and a business partner and the Sales Specialist gets the sale. And this happens just because he is who he is, with the skills and expertise that he has, and an outstanding desire to excel.

CHAPTER 3

SELECT A CUSTOMER VALUE PROPOSITION[2]

This book is about selling. It is designed to help sales professionals win more deals more often. But we believe that today's evolved sales professional is more than a bag-carrier or message communicator. Those salespeople who occupy the higher echelons of their profession are businesspeople, business professionals who sell.

Value creation is one of the basic tenets upon which a successful sales career is built. For a salesperson to excel, he needs to understand his market and the unique advantage he brings his customer. He must develop a strategy to succeed, and then marshal the resources required to guarantee successful execution of his strategy. The superior sales professionals we have encountered view themselves as proprietors of their own businesses, concerning themselves with measurement of the value they deliver to their employers, their customers and themselves. A book on selling would be flawed without the inclusion of that very topic that underpins the first principle of **SELECT SELLING**, that of selecting your customer. Coupled with expression of a unique differentiated value that the customer cares about, this principle can be the catalyst for unparalleled revenue acceleration in your chosen market.

This chapter addresses strategic marketing applied on an individual customer basis. In our opinion, going after a market strategically is not solely the purview of the corporation; it belongs also in the hands of the salesperson. After all, he spends more time with customers than anyone

---

2 This chapter extends the accepted definition of the sales professional, and addresses issues normally beyond his remit. If you want to focus exclusively on sales execution, read the section, 'Select your Target Customer' and then move on to the next chapter.

else. That's the landscape on which we paint our perspective. To guide your efforts, we have developed some principles, models, and tools that will help you navigate your journey. Together, these will help you articulate your vision, align your activities, execute effectively and productively, select a market and then dominate it. Crafted from the sales person's viewpoint, this chapter describes the creation of a Customer Value Proposition Statement to put the most pertinent parts of strategic marketing in your hands. The stages, shown in **Figure 5**, are:

1. Target Customer Selection.
2. Customer Value Proposition.
3. Addressable Market Size.
4. Competitive Differentiation.

FIGURE 5: STAGES IN CREATING A CUSTOMER VALUE PROPOSITION STATEMENT

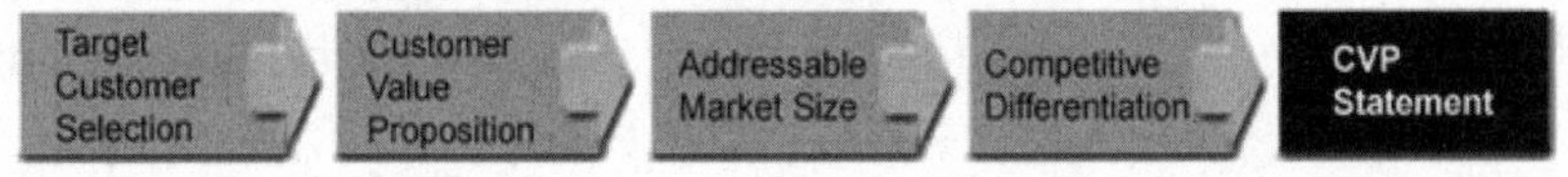

SELECT YOUR TARGET CUSTOMER

Analysis begins with understanding the ideal profile of a prospective customer. If every sales or marketing activity began with one question, what should that question be? It's not 'what's our return on investment, or ROI?'. It should never be 'what can we sell to this market segment?'. Before anything else is considered, you must determine what profile customer can benefit best from what you've got. What's your 'sweet spot'? Where does your offering mesh so smoothly with the customer's business requirement that he would be foolish not to consider purchasing your product, in preference to anything else? If your answer to that question doesn't direct you to a sufficiently profitable market segment, then you've got a problem with your offering, and you need to address it.

FIGURE 6: CVP STAGE 1: TARGET CUSTOMER SELECTION

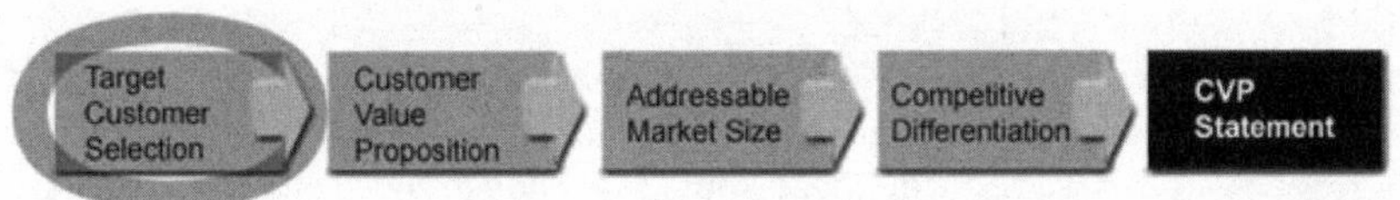

Selecting your target customer with restraint and accuracy will shorten your sales cycle. Your time is spent where it counts. Disciplined customer selection will increase the ROI for sales effort, reduce the marketing and support expenditure associated with the sale and, as a result, deliver greater profits. A single professional salesperson will be more effective addressing a market or territory armed with a well-aimed rifle, than an army of marketing folks wielding shotguns. Too often, we see companies adopting a 'spray and pray' attitude to business development. That is certainly a recipe for sub-optimal performance. How can you apply your solution to a customer's problem, unless you have focused on the needs of that specific customer? It's not possible. Is it more likely that you will succeed if you identify the ideal candidate, before you start your selling exercise? Without question!

Where's your 'Sweet Spot'?

We use the following six profilers (see **Figure** 7) to help our clients identify their ideal target customer. We call it the 'sweet-spot'.

1. Industry Segment.
2. Position on Technology Adoption Life Cycle.
3. Business Discipline.
4. Budget or Annual Spend.
5. Key Decision-maker.
6. Key Customer Need.

Do you know the attributes that would help identify a valid prospect? A true prospect is a prospective customer, not just a customer you'd like to have, not a brand-name account you want to use in your subsequent marketing, and certainly not someone who finds your technology interesting – but not just right now.

FIGURE 7: THE SELECT SELLING 'SWEET SPOT' INDICATOR

Indicator	Explanation
Industry Segment	Choose the industries, or industry sectors in which you will specialize. These should be chosen by considering the combination of (1) their propensity to buy, (2) the relative profitability of the sector (to you) and (3) the competitive landscape. You should include 'environmental' factors in this assessment – for example, regulatory compliance.
Position on Technology Adoption Life Cycle	Leading edge technologies require leading edge buyers. Early adopters of new technology offerings typically will be found in the technology or telecommunications sectors. Utilities companies, and governmental entities, are usually quite risk-averse. Match the customer profile to your position on the TALC. If the customer has a track record of being a technology laggard, then there is no point in approaching him with a leading edge solution.
Business Discipline	If your product offers cost savings, customers who are focused on operational efficiency may be more suitable targets than those who espouse a customer intimacy discipline, and the converse is also true. This test can equally apply to hard economic times or budget cuts *versus* high growth times or an expansionist mindset.
Budget or Annual Spend	The budget (in financial and/or human resource terms) that a customer has for the business area to which your solution applies is a good indicator of the company's suitability as a target customer.
Key Decision-maker	When your product requires significant behavioral change in your customer's organization, or is viewed as strategic, then you'd better be talking to a senior executive.
Key Customer Need	What is the one, single requirement that you want the customer to be focused on in the context of your (type of) solution? Is it process improvement, cost savings, convenience, etc?

One of our clients provides a product to help travelers use the Internet to book travel online. The product pulls together a multitude of flight choices, accommodation offerings, and car rental options, and presents it to the traveler. Costs associated with booking the flights are a fraction of the comparable costs incurred using a traditional travel agency. Because the product is presented as a service over the Internet, it is available 24 hours a day, every day, and all of the trips booked for a company get aggregated, to provide travel and expense management reporting to the finance department in that company.

Is this a solution that every company could use? Certainly any company with multiple travelers could benefit. But, like many technology solutions that are innovative and new, not all companies will choose to adopt the technology immediately. The main benefits of the solution, over traditional travel agencies, are 24/7 availability over the Internet, centralized real-time reporting, and significant cost savings achieved through reduced booking fees. Now that the airlines have stopped paying the travel agents commission, it has become necessary for the travel agency to charge their clients a booking fee per trip. Online travel booking solutions are threatening that revenue. But there will always be a need for a fully personalized service for certain complex trips, where the value of an experienced travel agent comes to the fore.

Our client had a field sales force and a telesales team. We worked with them to refine their target customer selection criteria for the field sales force. Together we developed a set of on-target criteria, and identified the off-target indicators, against the six sweet spot indicators.

Industry Segment

We wanted to understand which industries were more likely to adopt an online solution than retain the existing relationship with the offline travel agency. Clearly some sectors would be more comfortable with technology (for example, computer hardware or software companies) than others. Some would be more focused on the savings to be gained, either because they operated in tight-margin sectors, or because their focus was heavily financially-driven.

Our on-target criteria for selecting customers by industry pointed us towards technology companies, for their technology awareness, and the manufacturing sector, because of their cost focus. Sectors that we considered off-target included financial services, government and non-profit organizations. For a variety of reasons, we concluded that none of these would be rushing online, some would be less focused on costs savings, and others would still be hanging onto the personal service provided by a traditional travel agency.

Position on Technology Adoption Life Cycle

With all industry analysis, there is a danger of generalization, so we looked at the profile of the company, with respect to their position on the technology adoption life cycle. Our hypothesis was that, even if a company fell within our off-target sectors, they might still be valid prospects, if they stood out among their peers as heavy users of technology. Conversely, companies in an on-target industry might need to be red-flagged, if their technology usage was below the norm.

We developed a set of questions to determine the 'tech-savvy-ness' of a target. Is email used as the main correspondence mechanism? Does the company have a widely used intranet? Do executives list their cell-phone numbers on their business cards? Does the company use the Internet to do business with its customers? We felt that heavy users of technology would have a higher propensity than the technology laggards to move their travel bookings online.

Business Discipline

One of the key benefits of the proposed solution was described as a dramatic reduction in costs, so we determined that we should look to companies that focused on operational efficiency as their primary business discipline. Again, that pointed us towards the manufacturing sector, which continuously strives to drive costs out of the business. A customer-intimate business discipline was an anathema for our business development activities, as the companies in this category would be less concerned than their more frugal counterparts, about saving money on a trip.

Budget or Annual Spend

As we explored the various deal sizes that the sales-force was pursuing, we determined that the company's 'sweet spot' was in mid-range companies. Small companies weren't worth the effort of the cost of sale. Very large companies were likely to have an infrastructure in place that included their own travel department, with executives so high up in the stratosphere that they wouldn't be inclined to book their own travel online, no matter how easy it was.

Key Decision-maker

And that brought us to the decision-maker criterion. If the business sponsor was identified as a senior executive in the company, then the likelihood of a deal was increased, because they were negotiating for their own activity as well as that of the rest of the travelers in their company. If, however, the decision resided within the travel department, we concluded that the required level of behavior change was too great for this stage of the market. We recommended that our client should focus on companies outside of the Fortune 1000.

Key Customer Need

And finally to the buyers' perspective: what did the customers really want? If they wanted to be taken care of as they traveled the world, then self-service online wouldn't be high on their agenda. However, if 24/7 access, tools in the hands of the traveler, or cost savings made their list as high priority items, then we felt that the company was a real prospect for our client. We provided guidance to the sales and marketing teams to probe early for answers to these questions.

Each of these six indicators can help identify where you should spend your time. If you create your own version of the SELECT SELLING Sweet Spot Indicator, you will waste less time on fruitless activity. The following table will help you get on your way.

The SELECT SELLING **Sweet Spot Indicator Worksheet** is included in the **Appendix**; you can also download it at www.selectselling.com.

Vista.com is a leading provider of eBusiness solutions to small business. Simply put, Vista makes it easy for small businesses to develop their own complete website and secure ecommerce solution, using Vista's infrastructure. For example, a small flower shop might use Vista's solution to provide its customers with the ability to order flowers online. In return, the small business owner pays Vista a monthly fee.

At first glance, the market seems huge. The number of small businesses in the US alone is more than 20 million. By any independent analysis, that's a large market and maybe a large opportunity. However, the size of the market is itself a challenge. John Wall, the CEO of Vista, decided that the only way he could profitably get to the market was to leverage the reach of larger entities, like banks or trade associations, who already had an extensive customer base of small businesses. John selected his primary customer target as a large company who could provide him with a route to market. He engineered his product, and business model, to suit his large company partners, so that it would be easy for them to make Vista's solution available to their customers. His value proposition is then designed to meet the needs of his business partners.

> *Vista.com makes it possible for companies to quickly, easily and cost-effectively deliver replicated web services to large networks of businesses or locations.*
>
> *The value and benefits to our partners extends to all aspects of business ... from reaching new markets ... to adding value to offerings ... to growing revenue, loyalty and brand recognition.*
>
> *Vista.com delivers the applications (both front and back end) and open platform that help you meet the needs of the small business market, strengthen your relationships, extend your reach and branding and maximize revenues.*

It's a clear focus, for a defined market, and John aligned every aspect of his company's activities, to support that direction. The messages in his value statement specifically identify what will be delivered to his customers: cost-effectiveness, revenue growth, loyalty and brand recognition.

His discipline and focus was rewarded in early 2004 when SAM'S CLUB, a division of Wal-Mart Stores, chose Vista as their supplier of choice, to serve the needs of the SAM'S CLUB membership. SAM'S CLUB is the largest warehouse chain in the United States, providing services to small business owners and operators serving more than 46 million entrepreneurs and consumers. Seems like a well-targeted customer.

THE CUSTOMER VALUE PROPOSITION

Once you know who your customer is, the next step is to describe the value that your product delivers. The question we want answered now is whether anybody wants what you've got. Your first task is to describe, in terms the customers understand, why someone should care about your offering. This is your Customer Value Proposition, or CVP.

FIGURE 8: CVP STAGE 2: CUSTOMER VALUE PROPOSITION

Customers care about a product's benefits – not its features. You should too. It's not that the technology, or innovation, that's at the core of your product isn't important; it's just that, unless it delivers value to a customer, it doesn't matter. It's not that your lower price isn't advantageous; it's just that, until you create value in the mind of the buyer, the buyer isn't interested and any price is too high. That's the power of a well-crafted value proposition. It expresses your unique value, and gets the customer interested – it's your promise to deliver.

> A recent client of ours had innovative technology. It embedded the heart of a cell-phone into the body of a still, or motion, camera. You could send the camera anywhere that had cell-phone coverage, and, from any Internet station, watch the images it captured. A leading application for this technology is mobile security operations in vehicles.
>
> Larry, who was the CEO of the company, struggled with understanding why he was having difficulty gaining market acceptance. "It's really advanced technology. Why can't they understand that?". On examination, Larry's value proposition was purely feature-driven; pointing to Larry's engineering background: "Our product uses IP and GPRS to send digitized video streams over wired or wireless IP networks." It's short, encapsulates the key technologies being used, but does not explain the value.
>
> You may remember that the first software company to be listed on the New York Stock Exchange was Cullinet Software, the provider of the leading database system for IBM mainframe computers. Cullinet was

founded by John Cullinane, one of the early pioneers of the software industry. We were fortunate enough to have John as an investor and board member of a company we owned in the 1990s. John had a simple, yet effective, approach to getting a value proposition started. "Just imagine", John would say, in his Boston accent, "that you are placing a full page ad in the *New York Times* explaining your product. It must be simple, maybe no more than 25 words, and you should think about starting it with 'It is the first/only ...'." This simple approach, from John, can guide you to uncover the uniqueness in your product or service.

Perhaps using John's approach, Larry might have come up with a better description for his product - perhaps: "We are the first company to have combined a cell-phone and a video-camera, so that, over the Internet, you can visually track things that move large distances, which is something a fixed camera, or webcam, cannot do". That's a better message. Customers can easily understand why they might be interested in what Larry's got - they may need to be able to track a fleet of vehicles visually in real-time - and can determine for themselves whether they attach any significance or value to the benefits described.

As you develop your CVP, you need to ask yourself what benefit your product delivers. Does it make an existing process more effective, thereby increasing revenue for the customer? Will it deliver cost-efficiencies? It must do one or the other. Based on your current market knowledge, will it be an urgent purchase for the customer in the short term? The last thing you want is to spend your time promoting something that the customer finds interesting, but doesn't feel the urgency to act on now.

The good news is that the number of problems your customer has is endless. Life in large corporations today is an endless struggle to improve, increase, transform or reduce. Your task is to determine which one, or two, of these problems you can solve, and what value you can deliver. Here are some possibilities:

- Increased revenues
- Decreased costs
- Increased market share
- Improved customer retention
- Faster response time
- Increased sales per customer
- Improved asset utilization
- Reduced cost of goods sold
- Faster time to market
- Improved operational efficiency
- Decreased employee turnover
- Increased differentiation
- Decreased operational expenses
- Reduced cost of sales
- Faster collections
- Minimized risk

- Additional revenue streams
- Improved time-to-profitability
- Reduced cycle time
- Faster sales cycles
- Increased market share
- Increased billable hours
- Increased inventory turns
- Reduced direct labor costs

It is useful to think about the value you deliver in terms of what we call 'measurable and ambient value'. Measurable value is tangible. 'Reduce response time by 30%', 'increase market penetration by 10%', 'reduce the labor costs by half', are all examples of measurable value, easily identified and easy to explain. Ambient value is hard to explain and harder to sell. 'Improved image' and 'stronger morale' are truly examples of ambient value. However, people often fall into the trap of describing their measurable value as ambient value. 'Better customer satisfaction' and 'increased productivity', unless quantified, are perceived as ambient value and that's hard to sell. Better customer satisfaction means a reduction in customer churn, while increased productivity brings lower production costs. Do the work, and run the numbers to quantify the benefit, and turn a perceived ambient value into a real, measurable one.

When you make CVP decisions, you will choose to emphasize certain features of your offering, and de-emphasize others. When you make any purchase decision, perhaps upgrading to a new cell-phone, moving house, renewing a magazine subscription, or buying the latest 1980s rock anthem CD, your purchase is guided by certain unique elements of the product offering. Be disciplined as you develop your CVP. You need to uncover the unique elements of your product that customers will value enough to part with their cash – and that's where you focus.

The following five questions will help you define that area of focus:

- Who is the real buyer?
- What is the impact of your product on the buyer's company?
- What are the [ranked] purchase criteria of the buyer that arise from his perception of how your [type of] product might impact his organization?
- What are the existing and potential sources of unique value that you can deliver – what's your special 'sauce'?
- How do you know your sauce is special and that the customer cares?

If you're having difficulty figuring out for yourself how to best explain your value, talk to some current or prospective customers, and ask them to describe the situation (and pain) that first motivated them to buy your product. Check with industry analysts, such as the Gartner Group, to understand the customer trends they see in your marketplace. Get your own customers to describe, in their own words, what they see as the value in your offering. Ask them how they would describe your company to someone else in their industry. Listen carefully to what they have to say, test it for yourself, and refine your pitch, incorporating the pain points and description that they have outlined.

In 1999, when salesforce.com started life, it began with a singularly clear vision: 'Deliver sales force automation software as a service over the Internet'. Publicly taunting the large Customer Relationship Management (CRM) vendors, salesforce.com virtually chanted a mantra of 'the end of software' – a pointed jibe at its competitors, Siebel Systems and SAP, who charge large license fees for their software. Salesforce.com, by contrast, sells its product as a service, by subscription, over the web. When we visited the San Francisco office of salesforce.com in 2000, we were struck by how everyone in the company, in sales, marketing and product development, had a clear view of the company's immediate, and long-term, goals; in the short term, to be the leading player in Sales Force Automation delivered as a service over the Internet, and, in the longer term, to be the leading player in On-Demand CRM. The clarity of purpose guided all critical decisions. Everyone at the company knew what the company stood for. When the sales and marketing department initiated business development campaigns, there was no arguing over core market messaging. When the engineering team were faced with software development challenges, or technical architecture decisions, they could prioritize by determining which one helped them better deliver their software as a service. Every prospective customer understood what the company had to offer. Analysts and journalists could articulate the salesforce.com vision, nearly as well as salesforce.com's own employees. No confusion, no wasted cycles, clear focus and high productivity.

As we write this, salesforce.com has just been listed on the stock market with a valuation of more than $1 billion. This follows an achievement of almost $100 million in revenue in 2003. What is interesting about this, however, is that in many ways there was nothing very special about what salesforce.com had to offer, beyond its vision of software-as-a-service. Sales force automation software had been in existence for many years. Prior to the introduction of the salesforce.com product, alternatives such as ACT! and Goldmine provided similar functionality on a PC desktop. The paradigm shift was the Internet. It changed the laws of software distribution, and provided the opportunity for those with vision and focus to change the ground rules. The predecessors to salesforce.com had the capability – but didn't grab the customer's mindshare.

Around the same time as salesforce.com started, Siebel Systems introduced a similar online offering, but perhaps because of internal competition from its software license-based products, Siebel failed to deliver a clear vision to its customers. Siebel's challenge was how to succeed in a subscription-based software-as-a-service business without cannibalizing its software license revenue. It failed.

Salesforce.com had a vision and articulated it simply. The company executed on that vision in the market, while eschewing other opportunities that might dilute its strategic mission.

To increase the chance of emulating this success, companies must build their own strategic vision, and develop a complementary operational framework for their business. To attain substantial power in the market, you must achieve market leadership. To achieve market dominance, you must find a market where your value to the target customer is greater than all other players – and to pull that off, you must be self-critical, precise, rigorous and disciplined, about your product's value to your, carefully selected, market segment.

Addressable Market Size

You have now identified the specific benefit, which your product delivers, that will bring dramatic gain to a particular profile of customer. Next, you have to figure out whether there are enough of those types of customers, whom you can access, to make the target market worthwhile. This is your addressable market. So, now you're thinking – the bigger the market the better, right? Well, not necessarily. If you want to be a leader in your market – and that should be your goal – the fewer competitors you have, then the greater chance you have to lead, the lower the cost of sale, and the larger the profit margins. Unless you have very deep pockets, it makes a lot of sense to pick target markets that you can address in digestible chunks. Win in one niche first, and then move to a closely aligned niche and compete there.

FIGURE 9: CVP STAGE 3: ADDRESSABLE MARKET SIZE

One of the common mistakes made by young companies is that they develop their business plans based on the size of the total potential market. Then, they work on the assumption that they can get a small percentage of that large market. It rarely works that way, and you must be careful. Optimism, though necessary, can be terminal, and must be marshaled by a real-world sanity check.

In early 2004, we were engaged by a search engine company that was looking at the European Internet search market. At that time, the number of searches conducted globally on the Internet each month exceeded six billion! In Germany, France and the UK alone, we estimated that the aggregate number of monthly searches was just short of one billion. As you will surely have noticed, search results are increasingly populated with paid inclusions or accompanied by context-sensitive ads. Each click costs the advertiser up to 40 cents and about a third of searches return commercial results. At first glance, this looks like a potential market of $133 million per month - which translates to $1.6 billion annually.

As no money is made until someone clicks through on the ad, we applied a click-through percentage of (the industry average) 25%, reducing the annual market size to $400 million. Now, that's the total available market, but how much of that market could our client get? To figure that one out, we had to look at the profile of the market. Who are the major players? How is the advertiser serviced? What are the key dynamics that drive search revenue?

There are two main routes to market for a search engine company. Users tend to search the Internet, either by going to one of the main search engines, such as Google or Yahoo!, or by using the web search capability on their favorite website. For example, you will notice that the web search on CNN.com is provided by Yahoo!, while Earthlink's search capability is powered by Google. We call this the 'third-party distribution' market. As our client did not have the resources to compete with the large players (even if that was possible), we recommended the third party distribution market. Our rationale was that our client could win the hearts and minds of the 'second-tier' web sites who wanted a **true business partner** that could offer **more flexibility** and a **greater share** of the advertising revenue than either of the two big players (Google and Yahoo!).

As we continued our market-sizing exercise, we reduced the $400 million to exclude that part of the third party market owned largely by Google and Yahoo!. Then we profiled the target customer for our client. That ideal customer was the website owner in a large portal or publishing business; large enough to have significant site traffic, but not large enough to be a real target for Google or Yahoo! - in other words, those companies that managed websites with between one and 10 million searches per month. The culmination of our work resulted in identifying, by name, 300 specific targets across Europe, and a resultant addressable market opportunity of $55 million, with an estimated achievable market share of 20% in 2004, resulting in potential revenue of $11 million.

See what happened here? First we focused on those countries in Europe with the greatest Internet penetration. Then we identified the potential revenue from that market, recognized the competition, and picked a segment that our client could address, win and sustain. Six months on, it looks like our client is on track for about $14 million this year - a little over our number - directly from the specifically identified customers.

To determine the addressable market, you first have to define the profile of a customer, or company, to whom your product, as described by your CVP, delivers optimum value. Companies may be selected by territory, industry, revenue, number of employees, existing technology infrastructure, or other guidelines. Then it's a simple calculation.

Your addressable market (AM$) is equal to the total number of target customers selected to meet your ideal profile (N), multiplied by the average value of the sale (V$), and, finally, multiplied by the percentage of customers (C%), likely to purchase in a given year:

AM$ = N x V$ x C%

That's the addressable market. Next, you must figure out the competitive uniqueness that you can deliver to your potential customers in order to maximize your share of that addressable market.

If you're a sales person, with a territory and quota, you need to do this exercise for yourself, firstly to figure out whether there is enough opportunity for you to make your number, and secondly to determine, from a competitive perspective, what percentage of deals you need to win against the other competition, to be the leader in your territory.

Competitive Differentiation

Competitive differentiation must be at the heart of your strategic framework. How you select, deliver and articulate, what's different about your offering, will impact the sustainability of your business activity. It's about creating, and sustaining, superior performance founded on a cost advantage, a unique benefit delivered at a premium price, or a strategic alignment with your market's needs. We described earlier how your uniqueness must be part of your customer value proposition, or CVP. Your CVP must include the 'what' that's different. We focus here on the 'how' – how you create that difference.

Figure 10: CVP Stage 4: Competitive Differentiation

Differentiation is successful if you can be better (than your competitors) at something that your customers value. Just being different doesn't mean you're differentiated, and differentiation is only valuable if it is sustainable. This requires that the cost of maintaining your differentiation is not too high, and that your uniqueness cannot be easily replicated, or substituted, by your competitors.

The starting point is always the buyer, and his perspective of value. You can create value for your customer to justify a premium price or preferential (competitive) vendor status, either by reducing the total buyer costs for an activity or by increasing his performance.

Reducing total buyer cost can be achieved in many ways. For example, reducing usage costs by enabling consumers to conduct their banking online, reducing consumables costs in inkjet printers with refillable cartridges, reducing risk with superior warranties, reducing software integration costs with inclusion of industry standard programmable interfaces. As you seek to reduce the cost of an activity for your customer, you must understand how your offering impacts the customer's value chain, and how it may be used with other products or activities in his company.

Increasing the customer's performance depends on the type of customer, and what constitutes optimum performance levels. If your customer is a bank, the buyer may measure performance by how your products help him serve his customer. There are many ways of increasing the buyer's performance: increasing the organization's communication through the introduction of an intranet, increasing sales revenue by providing an add-on product opportunity, increasing customer service responsiveness through a CRM system, increasing compliance with compliance management software, or increasing delivery effectiveness through outsourced logistics management.

Competitive differentiation is only valuable if the buyer understands what's different, and why he should care. In some cases, you may need to modify your sales process or nudge the customer's buying process to implant the uniqueness of your offering with a chosen individual in the buyer's organization. A highly technical product may well be better understood by the company's engineering staff, rather than by the business sponsor who will use your product. To drive home the value of your uniqueness, you may need to change how you interact with the customer: involve a technical sales engineer in the sale, provide evaluation materials for the customer to compare your product with that of your competitors, or provide a trial version of the product to position it with those who will best value the differentiation you deliver.

Four Types of Product Features

To determine who you need to interact with at the buyer's organization, it may help to think about the features of your product in the following terms. They can generally be categorized into four types:

- The first type is called the **qualifier**, the mandatory feature necessary to qualify you as a contender. Email software must let you send and receive email. The basic requirement of an online banking system is that users can access their bank account information over the Internet. Word-processors should have basic formatting capabilities and editing functions. These mandatory features are taken for granted, and the customer expects that all vendors will meet this minimum threshold.
- Then there are what we call the **MEGOs** (my eyes glaze over), the features that manufacturers or vendors think are really cool, but the customer just doesn't like or care about. When this gets to uncontrolled proportions, it can lead to dramatic product failures. This happened to Apple: the first real PDA available was the Apple

Newton Messagepad, which could have been Apple's PalmPilot. However, its use centered on handwriting recognition, a feature that just didn't work well enough for customers. The product bombed.

- Next up are the **irritants**, those elements of your product that irritate the customer – but not enough to reject your product or make them defect as a customer. Microsoft's operating system products are frequently the target of complaints, because of real, or perceived, security vulnerabilities. In most cases, it doesn't stop corporations from standardizing on the products.
- Finally, there is the **special sauce**, that element of what you offer that really gets the customer excited. This is where you need to focus your attention when developing your CVP. Translate those special sauce features into benefits. Southwest Airlines is a *low-cost* airline. Linux is an *open* operating system. Nextel pioneered *push-to-talk* capability on its cell-phones. Salesforce.com delivers sales force automation *software-as-a-service* over the Internet.

Once you have identified your competitive differentiator, you have to ensure that you have all the resources you need, to deliver the full benefit to the customer. Can you execute on your promise to deliver, or do you need help? If you look around the world at the most successful technology companies, you will see each looking to partners to support their activities. Microsoft is reliant on software development companies to implement its .NET solution for customers. Dell leverages its logistics suppliers to deliver your customized PC to your door. Nokia depends on its telecommunications partners and retail outlets to reach its target audience. SAP needs systems integrators and consultants to provide a complete solution to its customers.

It's no use having the best core product in the world if there are still bits missing in the solution that make it hard for the customer to buy or implement. If you have an incomplete solution, or it's hard to adopt, two things can happen and they're both bad (see **Figure 11**):

- If your product is easy to adopt, but provides little benefit, you're in an unsustainable, price-led business.
- If the product provides significant benefit, but is hard to adopt and servicing the customer is difficult, then your product levels will suffer and it'll be hard to scale your business.

FIGURE 11: THE SELECT SELLING COMPLETE SOLUTION MODEL

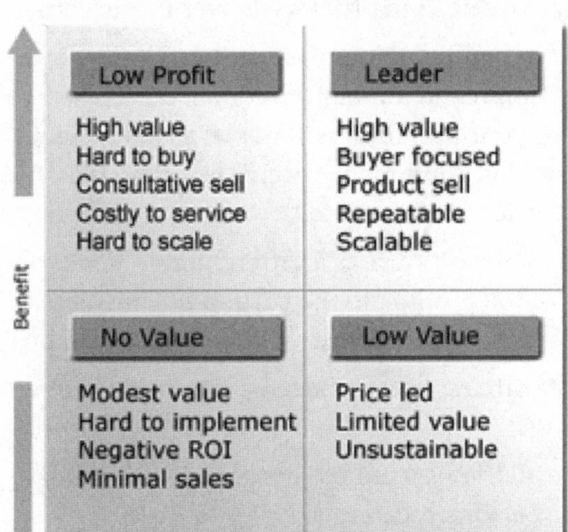

And, if the product provides little value, and is hard to adopt, then you're clearly wasting everyone's time. But, if your product has the potential to deliver high value, you must ensure that you can make it easy for the customer to adopt it. Find the help he needs, and either provide it yourself or engage a partner to assist.

Make It Stick

Although you've figured out what's different about what you've got, it's only valuable if you can make it stick. Is your competitive differentiation sustainable? There is always the possibility that the customer's requirements will change, or that someone else might provide your special sauce. Whether it is proprietary intellectual property, dramatic cost advantage, or heavy switching costs, you must create a large barrier to entry for your competitors. Your differentiation must be significant.

If you're a small company, getting this right is the difference between success and oblivion.

Here's what *not* to do:

- Don't base your differentiation on something the customer doesn't want. Remember the Apple Newton.

- Don't make it too differentiated. If product functionality exceeds customer requirements, it will be difficult to get the customer to pay the premium you need in order to deliver those features profitably.
- Don't forget to highlight your uniqueness. While you may occasionally command a premium for an 'advertised value' that you don't deliver, your premium will not be sustainable. Conversely, however, you will continue to receive less than the product deserves if you don't articulate the value.
- Don't focus on the product as a differentiator. Focus on the application of the product to the customer's business as the differentiator – how the product will be used in the business.
- Don't deliver differentiators that cost you more than you get in return.
- You can't be all things to all buyers at the same time, so don't forget to 'select the customer' carefully.

One of the industries most impacted by the Internet in recent years has been the travel sector. Travelers are clicking in droves, booking trips online, and offline travel agencies are going out of business faster than you can count. The big players in online travel are Expedia, Orbitz and Travelocity and competition is fierce. Within this segment, one area that has yet to be won is business travel, and it is, as yet, largely the preserve of offline agencies. Historically, companies have a relationship with a travel agency that manages all of the details for a company's executives and other travelers. Now, in mid-2004, the potential for significant cost savings is beginning to build some momentum, as the corporate travel sector is starting to move online. The value proposition, to the corporate travel market, is presented differently by each of the three major competitors.

- **Expedia Corporate Travel:** Expedia Corporate Travel is a full-service corporate travel agency. Enjoy the services of world-class travel agents dedicated to your business, plus leading-edge online travel planning and booking tools in one easy-to-use solution.
- **Orbitz for Business:** We're a full-service online travel agency designed to help companies with 10 to 10,000 employees and $50,000 to $50 million in travel expenses reduce overall travel costs, streamline operations and save valuable time and resources.
- **Travelocity Business:** Saving money on business travel has never been easier. Travelocity Business is an entirely new way for businesses to plan, buy and manage their employees' travel, offering all the cost savings, service and features you need.

The features that make an online travel agency attractive are (1) cost savings (typically transaction fees for online bookings are about 20% of the cost of an offline agent), (2) 24/7 access, and other Internet accessibility related benefits and (3) easy-to-use booking tools. The major disadvantage perceived by business travelers is that they don't receive the same level of care and attention. Given that background, which of the three players do you think presents the best message?

Based solely on these descriptions, Expedia and Orbitz seem to suggest themselves to specific markets. If Expedia can deliver on the service promise, at a reasonable price, the proposition is attractive to those companies moving from the offline agency world, delivering an online experience - supported with service. Orbitz seems to be the low-cost option, and if price is a customer's prime motivation, then Orbitz is a strong contender. Based on its value proposition alone, Travelocity appears to be in second place, whether the customer is looking for best service, or lowest cost.

Expedia likely has the edge over Orbitz today, given that the emotional concern of travelers probably outweighs the efficiency argument put forward by Orbitz. The great challenge for Expedia, if it is to succeed in the corporate travel market, will be to resist the temptation to try to force its corporate business model into its very successful leisure travel model too soon. The leisure travel business is all about operational efficiency, but corporate travelers prefer to deal with a company that espouses a customer-centric strategy.

The Customer Value Proposition Statement

Technology's continuous state of rapid evolution and dynamic market conditions places severe stress on those technology companies striving for survival, success and, ultimately, hyper-growth. Almost by definition, the technology sector is ever-changing. New products, trends, and increasing levels of customer sophistication, combine to create a Darwinian environment, where only the fittest survive. To stay alive, a company must have a proposition that delivers value and is sustainable. It must have the resources, ability, and desire to design and execute a plan to deliver on that proposition. The delivery of superior value to some market segment, through increased benefits – at a competitive price – lies at the core of any successful business.

For the professional salesperson, his world is a microcosm of his company's. The same issues apply, though at a more granular level. Clarity of purpose, a laser-like focus on execution, an uncluttered vision of implementation strategies and tactics, and identification of prospective partners and allies, are essential ingredients when defining the recipe for achievement. If ambiguity or fuzziness exists, or if the correct offering is not being provided to the right customers, through the optimum channels, sustained success is impossible.

It is very helpful if you can create a short Customer Value Proposition Statement to articulate your value. This delivers the clarity you need, to communicate with your friends, colleagues and customers.

FIGURE 12: CVP STAGE 5: CREATING A CUSTOMER VALUE PROPOSITION STATEMENT

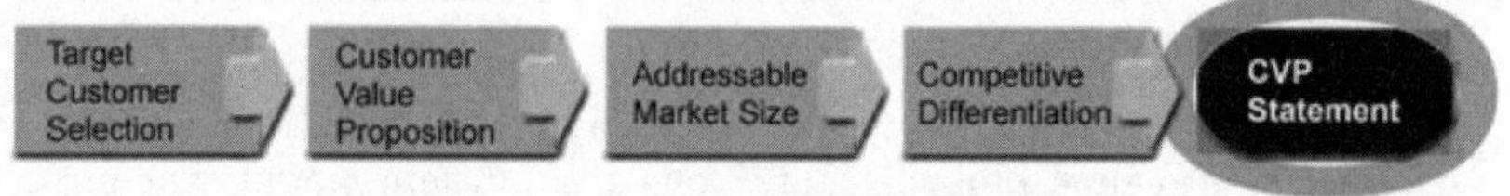

Figure 13 suggests six steps to create a CVP statement, while **Figure 14** gives an example of a CVP Statement, based on our own company.

FIGURE 13: STEPS IN CREATING A CUSTOMER VALUE PROPOSITION STATEMENT

#	Name	Description
1	**High Level Description**	This should be your short description that, in 25 words or less, identifies your market and describes what your company does for your target customer.
2	**Benefit Statement**	Outline the benefits that you can promise to deliver to your target customers
3	**Customer Pain**	What is the compelling reason for the customer to buy your service or product? Describe his business problem or pain.
4	**Buyer Description**	Within the target company, you must be able to decide the profile of the likely buyer.
5	**Differentiation**	What makes you different? Why should the customer decide to do business with you rather than with your competitor?
6	**Delivery Mechanism**	Describe how the product or service is delivered to the customer. This may include reference to your distribution channel strategy, your own network of offices or your delivery partners.

If you want to use this template to build your own strategic value proposition, a softcopy of the template is available for you to download at www.selectselling.com.

Our consulting business is called International Ventures. This is our primary activity outside of our educational services and it's where we spend most of our time. **Figure 14** shows the strategic value description that we use to provide clarity to our employees and customers. We provide it here as an example that you might like to review. We'd be delighted if you can suggest ways that we could improve it!

FIGURE 14: AN EXAMPLE CVP STATEMENT

High Level Description	International Ventures helps technology companies grow revenue through definition and implementation of organizational process – from strategic market positioning to sales execution.
Benefit Statement	Our clients gain effective, pragmatic and scalable solutions that reduce selling cycles, cost of sales, and market entry costs; and increase organizational alignment, sales conversion rates, revenue and profit.
Customer Pain	Growing a technology company is a challenge. Products are hard to describe and value is difficult to explain. Traditional sales techniques are ineffective. Selling cycles are long and customers have complex buying processes.
Buyer Description & Differentiation	Through 'experience-based' strategic sales and marketing consulting and knowledge transfer services, we help the leadership of technology companies grow revenue from the inside out. Unlike traditional consulting companies, our executives are seasoned entrepreneurs, marketing strategists and sales professionals. Each one knows what it takes to be successful because they have been there themselves.
Delivery	With representation in the US and Europe, International Ventures is uniquely equipped to help its clients serve either or both markets.

The Message is the Medium

It surprises us how often CEOs unconsciously relinquish the responsibility of message delivery to the salesforce, without providing them with assistance or the tools to ensure consistent presentation of that message. Salespeople are often left to figure out for themselves the customer value proposition in the context of an individual buyer. Marketing will sometimes confuse marketing communications with strategic marketing and it's not surprising to see that the value being articulated in sales proposals created by the successful sales professional bears little resemblance to the messaging content in marketing collateral on the company's website. After all, how much time are the marketing executives spending with the customers?

Today's evolved sales professionals, the Sales Specialists described in the previous chapter, are taking upon themselves a strategic marketing perspective, at an individual customer level, and in this case it is certain that the medium is truly the message.

CHAPTER 4

THE BUYER'S PERSPECTIVE

When speaking to a senior purchasing professional recently, we were reminded of the extent of the 'perspective gap' between the buying community and the selling community. As he guided his organization through the process of many purchase cycles, he invested a lot of time in educating his team about how to handle vendors; counseling never to allow themselves build too close a relationship with the sales person; coaching internal technical and business team members how to handle vendors' positioning tactics during the evaluation and selection process; using competitive pressures to keep suppliers focused; and managing the communication process between the suppliers and his company, to make sure that he could control the procedure. This included keeping senior executives away from vendors, and forbidding access to these executives until his chosen point in the cycle. He had strong views on capped licensing fees, milestone-based payments, and using strong positive and negative financial motivators to provide suppliers with adequate incentives to deliver on time and within budget.

As we examined his process and procedures, we couldn't find anything that was unfair or unreasonable. All vendors got the same information, were given the same presentation opportunities and time to prove their value, and all unsuccessful bidders were given a full and frank debrief immediately after the selection process. The striking thing about this process, however, was the level of built-in planning. Professional buyers know every step they want to take in the buying cycle. They have a detailed project plan, with hurdles and obstacles you have to scale, and unless you can visualize the journey they want to take, and you have your own map to get there, you won't be with them when they reach their destination.

In this chapter, we will look at the corporate buying process and the evolved professional buyer. We will examine the multiple roles played by different influencers in the buying process and consider how we might address the concerns of each of these players. We will then look at the different stages of the buying cycle and consider how to align selling activities to each of these stages, recognizing the different emotions at play.

THE CORPORATE BUYING PROCESS

A typical buying process in a large corporation is a (sometimes unnecessarily) complex thing (see **Figure 15**). Your job is to be part of the process as early as you can. Projects start because a Line of Business (LOB) Manager has identified a business need – a problem to be solved. If you helped him realize or articulate that need, you're ahead of the game. You might lose this opportunity to internal competition, but if you have not been involved thus far, you won't even know you have missed an opportunity and you certainly won't have the chance to influence the outcome of any 'build-*vs*-buy' deliberations.

FIGURE 15: THE CORPORATE BUYING PROCESS

Identify need
Sponsor
High level requirements
Sponsor
Detailed requirements
Sponsor +
Approve project
Sponsor, Fin +
Research market
Team
Agree approach
Team
Approach RFI/RFP
Team
Evaluate and select
Team
Negotiate commercials
Contracts
Get final approval
Team
Award contract
Team
Manage delivery
Team

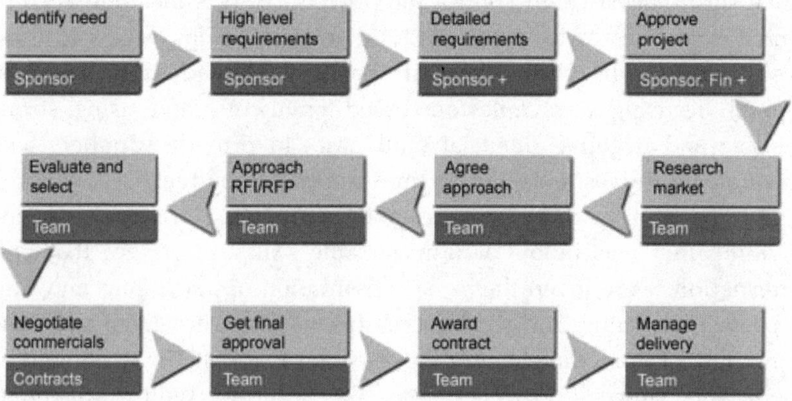

If the customer has decided to proceed, he will research the market to identify potential suppliers. The customer will ask market influencers and analysts to suggest potential suppliers. They will also conduct research via the Internet, and they will talk to their counterparts in other companies in their industry. If you're a Sales Specialist, you should be at the top of the list.

Using internal resources, or external consultants, the customer will now document his needs in detail and write a Request for Information (RFI), or Request for Proposal (RFP), to be distributed to vendors who meet pre-determined evaluation or selection criteria. (RFPs are mandatory for certain organizations, such as governmental entities.)

You should always beware of the unsolicited RFP! If the first time you hear about an opportunity is when you get the RFI or RFP document, you will rarely win the deal. It is more probable than not that some competitor has been involved in shaping the structure of the document to suit the strengths of his offering and that your involvement will be limited to making up the tender numbers required by the customer's purchasing procedures.

As responses to the RFP are received, the customer will likely have defined evaluation forms, scorecards and questionnaires to assist in arriving at an initial vendor list. As a candidate, you will then have the opportunity to make a presentation, and will be invited to present references for the customer to check on your track record. The customer will conduct his own risk analysis of each vendor, before conducting preliminary negotiations with each one who passes the requisite tests. Most large organizations will then settle on a final short list of two or three vendors, before making their final decision. Even if you are the final selected candidate, you are not over the finish line until the budget has been finally released, negotiations are completed and contracts are signed.

You must assume that the customer has a professional buying plan. Buyers have access to all the information they need about you, your product and your competitors and will commoditize as many purchases as they can – forcing suppliers to compete on price and leaving little room for differentiation. In all of the analysis we have done of deals lost, one of the common factors for the loss has been a lack of understanding of the customer's buying process. There is lots of evidence to suggest that, unless you understand the customer's plans, their real business needs, and can develop their needs to show your distinct competitive advantage and real business value, success is unlikely. It's much easier to design your selling plan, if you know the customer's buying plan.

The complexity and rigor of the professional buying process in large corporations can sometimes be advantageous to smaller vendors.

Though it is typically harder for small companies to get on 'preferred vendor' lists (they have some extra walls to climb to prove they are financially stable, reliable, and have a long-term future and vision), smaller companies also have an advantage. They can be more flexible, responsive and adaptable and can mold their selling process to mesh better with the customer's buying cycle, more easily than their less flexible larger competitors.

THE SIX BUYING INFLUENCER ROLES

Trying to understand who the buyer is in a large corporation is sometimes a bit like a Broadway production. Does the play have a cast of thousands or is it a one-man show? Who is playing what role? Who is the lead? How important is the supporting cast? Who's the real buyer? Is it the Chief Financial Officer who controls the money, or the CIO who sets the technology standards for the company? Is the Director of Purchasing, who manages the Preferred Vendor list, in a cameo role, or is he the star attraction? Maybe the star is the Line of Business (LOB) manager who has the business problem, or the End User who will end up using the product. In many companies, it may be all of these. In other organizations, the buying power is vested entirely in the LOB Manager. The factors determining who is involved include the state of market maturity for the product being purchased, the value of the purchase, and whether you are the incumbent supplier.

The complexity of the buying process is usually linked to the size of the deal. Bigger deals present greater risk for the customer, and consequently attract significantly more diligence in the process. Incumbent suppliers will already have scaled certain heights for the customer and will have had the opportunity to establish credibility and relationship with the buyer. It is frequently much harder for a company to purchase from a vendor who is not already an approved supplier, and customers will stick with their existing suppliers if they can show sustained performance.

Whether the buying process necessitates multiple players from the customer's organization will vary from one situation to the next. But, in every case, the *buying roles* will be constant. They may be vested in one or multiple individuals, but the same roles will exist in each instance. We have identified six roles you should cater for as you craft your sales plan for each opportunity. For the sake of clarity, we have personified the roles into six individuals who characterize the inherent attributes usually associated with the position:

- Line of Business Manager
- The User Buyer
- The Evaluator
- The Financial Buyer
- The Legal / Procurement Buyer
- The Internal Champion.

You should cultivate relationships with each of these 'centers of power'.

Line of Business Manager

The opportunity usually starts here. Depending on the size of the company, the LOB Manager will usually have a Vice President, General Manager, or Director title. He typically has functional responsibility for an area of the business, has general budget control over a pre-approved budget and is concerned with solving a particular business problem. This role is the center of pain. Uncovering that pain, the business problem, and the impact of the pain, is essential.

Assuming you can develop a good relationship with the LOB Manager, he will be a great ally during the selling process. He should be powerful enough to find extra budget if necessary, and facilitate access to all other layers in the organization.

The LOB Manager is an agent of change, has personal equity vested in the process and has right of entry to the centers of power in the company. If convinced of your value, he will sell throughout the organization for you – and you better not let him down.

The User Buyer

The User is concerned about the day-to-day operational issues of using your product and integrating the product into the business processes. He will have to live with your product, and will be anxious about its impact on productivity and his everyday life. His concerns are very personal. It's rare that a User can make a deal happen, but he can almost certainly stop it. His concerns will center on how easy the product is to use, what process changes are required for implementation, and what impact its adoption will have on job performance.

Users will need to be satisfied that training, documentation, reliability, support and service are more than satisfactory. They will need to feel comfortable with you and your post-sales support staff. Behavior and business process change issues will be to the forefront of their minds, and you must be mindful of that. Their buy-in is essential to a successful project and, if a key user buyer is not convinced, it will be very hard to close the sale.

The Evaluator

Less emotionally invested in the project, the Evaluator is not fundamentally interested in either the business issues or the ease of use of the product, though both topics carry weight in the evaluation. In a technology purchase, the Evaluator will likely reside in the IT department. His focus will be technical. His concerns will include the fit of your solution with existing in-house expertise.

If the technical aspects of your solution are not aligned with the standards of the customer's organization, you will need to marshal all your resources to assure the Evaluator that his support effort will not be disproportionate to the value you bring. Integration, performance, and standardization will all be high on his agenda. In many cases, the Evaluator may present as being the final decision-maker and it is important to probe this assertion deeply. If a business manager like the LOB Manager is involved in the purchase, it is more likely that the Evaluator assumes a similar role to that of the user – that of a gatekeeper and influencer – but at a higher level.

John was a client of ours who ran a software tools company. His company was one of the first providers of Windows development tools back in the 1990s. The company was very successful selling the product in the US and Europe. Customers were happy with the product, the service reputation was excellent, and users found the applications developed with the tool really easy to use.

Then Microsoft launched Visual Basic and let loose an overwhelming *tsunami* of developer conferences and marketing seminars, quickly establishing Visual Basic as the leading Windows development tool for many applications. Pretty soon, some of John's customers were telling him that, although they loved his product and their users were happy, the availability of trained Visual Basic programmers to employ meant that they were going to standardize on the Microsoft tool for future projects. The Evaluators, at the companies that were John's customers, had decided that Visual Basic would be the corporate standard - and that was the end of the road.

> John's story had a happy ending. He redesigned a particular feature of his product to work with Visual Basic, sold half a million licenses and went on to sell the company to a competitor.

The message however should be clear. The Evaluator has the power to kill your project or exclude you from new opportunities. This can happen if your technology either doesn't make the grade in performance or features, or doesn't fit in with the corporate strategy.

The Financial Buyer

The Financial Buyer will sometimes be the CFO or another member of the finance team, but it won't always be that way. Depending on the size of the deal, the nature of the company, the state of the company, the economic conditions, the perceived risk of the purchase or its impact on the organization, the financial buyer can be found to have different titles. After the dot-com crash, the subsequent nervousness in the market, and attendant slow economy, we saw more deals requiring CFO approval than ever before. LOB Managers, who used to have discretion over their approved budgets, needed to get independent authorization each time they wanted to make a capital investment. You must uncover where the sign-off authority really is, if you are to be sure you have identified the role accurately.

The focus of the Financial Buyer is almost always related to the bottom line. Sometimes it is top line, cash-flow or share price, but neglecting his bottom line analysis is something you do at your peril. The key question for the Financial Buyer will be return on investment. "If I spend a dollar, will I save or make money?" Final release of budget usually rests here, and this role is involved in 'green-lighting' a project. It also has veto power and can choose to re-allocate the budget to a competing project.

The Legal / Procurement Buyer

The job isn't over until the i's are dotted and the t's are crossed. While price negotiations will typically be a conversation between you and the LOB Manager or Financial Buyer, the detailed terms and conditions of a deal will often be controlled by the Legal Buyer. The devil is always in the detail. Service level agreements, penalty clauses, software escrow arrangements, payment terms, intellectual property ownership and indemnity, warranty and maintenance, confidentiality and trade secrets, exclusivity, performance guarantees, acceptance criteria, volume pricing, and employee solicitation agreements, are all items to be negotiated.

Depending on the company, the Legal Buyer or Procurement Officer may well co-ordinate the entire buying cycle. You should try to include him in your presentations and selling process, so that he is party to your value-selling activities. Otherwise, he will see his role exclusively as a protector of his company's commercial interests, to the certain detriment of your value and margin.

The Internal Champion or Coach

Unless you have someone on the inside that is on your side, it will be difficult to navigate all of the layers in a selling situation. You need an Internal Champion, someone to guide you, open doors, give you feedback on how you are doing, identify weaknesses or risks, and provide you with an honest assessment of the buyer's perspective on you, your product or service and your company. Sometimes, part of your role is to make the Champion look good. If he is working for you, pass him key information that will lend credibility to his position.

Sometimes one of the other roles doubles up as a Champion. The Evaluator may be a real fan of your technology. The LOB Manager might value your industry expertise, or the CFO as Financial Buyer could be a supporter because you have demonstrated cost savings in the past. The Champion must have real influence and be respected by his colleagues and you need to qualify the Champion to be sure that you're taking guidance from the correct source.

Your Role is Producer

As you engage with each of the influencers in an account, remember that all votes are not necessarily equal. Internal to the customer's company, some players will be in the ascendant while others will be in decline. The politics of this factor will sometimes be evident in the personal motivations you discover. Your role is to direct, persuade, and question as you involve all of the players. Identify the winners – and if you're successful in your search, hitch your wagon to the rising star.

MONITORING ACCESS: THE SELECT SELLING POWER GAUGE

The **SELECT SELLING** Power Gauge is used to track your contact with the buying roles in the account. Over the course of the sales cycle, you need to make sure that you continue to have access to all the centers of power. Too frequently, the level of access at the upper echelons of the power hierarchy wanes over the duration of the sales cycle. This weakens the control you have over the sales process and leaves room for a competitor to steal the opportunity by 'calling high' and negating the access you have at the lower levels.

Different influencers have different roles along the way. You need to be sure that you manage access to power appropriately to give yourself the opportunity to deal with the changing emotions at all stages and at all levels. The fact that a complex sale has a long sales cycle underlines the need for a tool like this. Continuous contact is necessary if you are to stay to the forefront of your customer's mind. That way you can catch those timing-induced opportunities that will advance the sale or unearth new business in an existing account.

The Power Gauge is an easy tool to use. In **Figure 16**, we have divided the sale into four phases of the buying cycle. We describe these in detail later in this chapter. For each named influencer or role, you should record each time you have meaningful contact with each individual. A quick look will identify gaps in your access to power.

The example Power Gauge in **Figure 16** shows a pretty healthy access record as we move through the first three phases of the buying cycle. Consistent contact with the Champion keeps you aware of your progress. Intermittent access to the Financial and Legal Buyer involves them in the process. The LOB Manager's engagement is fairly consistent, and should provide you with adequate opportunity to monitor his concerns continually and to drive home your value. The Evaluator and User are gatekeepers and, at this point in the process, you should have addressed any issues they might have, or at least be aware of further obstacles you need to tackle.

FIGURE 16: THE SELECT SELLING POWER GAUGE

Buying Cycle Phases ▶	Requirements			Evidence			Acquisition			Post-Sale		
LOB Manager: John S., VP Marketing	√	√	√		√		√	√	√			
User Buyer: Tony J., Joan C., ...			√	√	√	√	√	√	√			
Evaluator: Charles N.				√	√	√	√	√	√			
Financial Buyer: Patricia H., CFO				√				√	√			
Legal Buyer: Matt E., Snr. Dir. Procurement			√			√			√			
Internal Champion: Patrick F., Marketing Manager	√	√	√	√	√	√	√	√	√			

The Power Gauge is a useful tool to help you overcome a natural tendency to interact only with the individuals or roles involved in any particular phase. Continued monitored access will lessen the opportunity for a competitor to usurp your position, or diminish your advantage. Go to www.selectselling.com to download the SELECT SELLING Power Gauge template.

SHIFTING BUYER CONCERNS

Think about the last time you made a big purchase. Perhaps it was something really major like a house or a car, or maybe something less dramatic like a replacement set of golf clubs. As you begin researching your purchase, your emotions are deeply engaged and, while you're generally interested in making sure that whatever you are buying is within your price range, you're focused on your needs. Is the house in the right location and big enough to do all the entertaining you're planning? Can the technology in the new golf clubs compensate for a certain lack of technique, and you always needed a two-seater sports car anyway – right? You view the house, test-drive the car, or swing the club, and now you're a little more focused on the details. You're visiting schools, shops and other amenities in the area, making sure the house isn't overrun by termites, and investigating the structural integrity of that extra room that was added last year. You're reading the J.D. Power survey, checking the automobile insurance costs and considering the residual value of the car, all the while testing out the response to "Me? I drive a Porsche" in the singles bars, and wondering if Tiger Woods can drive the ball 300 yards with this club, is there any reason why you can't. Now, it's the time to make up your mind and sign up. "What, are you crazy – sign up to pay a prince's ransom every month for 30 years, just for a place to sleep – you must think I'm mad! Why would I pay the price of a small house for a car that only has two seats? Maybe I should get a few golf lessons before I spend that amount of money on a set of clubs. I'm really not that keen on the game anyway."

The buying process is a funny thing. People often use information and data after the fact, to rationalize the very personal emotional decisions made during the buying process. While this is certainly truer in personal consumer purchases than in the corporate buying process, it is important to understand the different legs of the journey that your customers will travel as they travel towards their buying decision. The emotional influences are still at play, even if they have been formulized or regularized through the corporation's procurement process. They can be described as the four phases of the buying cycle.

THE FOUR PHASES OF THE BUYING CYCLE

All though the professional buying cycle, buyers are concerned about risk and the price of your offering. They seek evidence that you are the best supplier, and need to be assured that you can meet their needs. However, the buyer's primary emphasis changes throughout the buying cycle and they focus on different concerns at different times. It is important to know where you are in the cycle and to understand what's occupying the buyer's mind at that time.

In a departure from traditional wisdom, we have segmented the buying cycle itself into four segments, to include Post-Sale activity for the sales professional. More than ever, a sales person's key asset is his customer, and it is our belief that he needs to be involved after the deal has been consummated, to maintain the relationship. In **Figure 17**, we chart the relative importance of each concern through the process (a full black circle represents high importance).

FIGURE 17: THE FOUR PHASES OF THE BUYING CYCLE

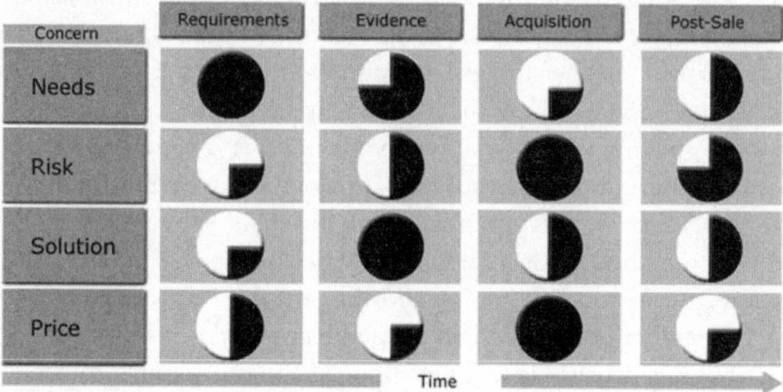

The stages in the buying cycle are:

1. Early in the procurement cycle, the buyer will briefly check on price to make sure your offering is in the general area of his expected budget. At this point, it's all about his needs, his wants and his process. Getting past the first checkpoint requires that you pass the first features test. Can your offering meet the needs of the customer? If not, the price doesn't matter. So far the customer has little risk, as no major irrevocable decisions are being made. This is the **Requirements** phase of the buying cycle. Your opportunity to shape the customer's requirements is strongest in this phase of the buying cycle. Refer to the chapter on Progressive Questioning later in the book to see techniques that you might use.

2. Leaving the Requirements phase behind and entering the **Evidence** phase, the customer now requires very specific data from you to substantiate your claims that you can meet the needs that he outlined. You must prove to him that your solution is all it's cracked up to be. As he invests more time, his risk is increasing but his focus remains pinpointed on your evidence. This will probably include detailed examination of your offering, reference calls to other customers, future support, product vision and more specific price discussions. Likely as not, the customer will reduce his list of potential suppliers at this time. It's still like buying a car or a house. You're down to a choice of two or three, all of which meet your needs, each with sufficient evidence to

assuage your concerns about whether you're getting everything you expect – but now you're getting a little nervous.

3. As the customer is making the final choice and is getting ready to sign on the dotted line, the purchase is at its most vulnerable, and the buyer is more nervous than at any other time in the cycle. Up to now, there is always a way out – but once the decision is made, it's done, over, complete. Better not screw up now. This is where the professional sales person understands the need for positive reinforcement and a restatement for the buyer of the rationale for the buying decision, which hopefully has been arrived at jointly. In this, the **Acquisition** stage, all the work done up to now can be for naught if the buyer get butterflies and isn't comfortable to proceed. Risk is uppermost in his mind, and price rears its head again. "So if I'm going do this, you need to give me a deal." Sometimes the buyer needs something extra, or a price concession, to make him feel good about making the decision and to help him over the line. This is particularly true when one person will carry the responsibility for making the decision.

4. Risk fades as a factor in the buyer's mind after the purchase is made, only to be replaced by anxiety. As they say, the proof of the pudding is in the eating, and until the new product or service has been fully implemented and bedded in, the buyer will still feel vulnerable. You must address that concern if you want to maintain a long-term relationship. **Post-Sale**, the buyer no longer cares about price. Real evidence is needed to prove to him that he made the right decision. Work hard at it, and reward his trust.

Knowing the buyer's perspective at each stage in the buying cycle, you can be extra conscious of the issues that will be to the forefront of his mind. You now have an opportunity to fully align your activities to the specific context of the particular buying phase.

EMBRACING THE BUYER'S PERSPECTIVE

For each buying phase, there are requisite selling actions to be taken. If you embrace the buyer's perspective, these actions become clear. In the following chapter we describe some techniques, using the **SELECT SELLING** Progressive Questioning Control Model (see **Chapter 5**), which will help you to illuminate the path you need to travel.

Let's first understand the four stops along the road:

- Requirements.
- Evidence.
- Acquisition.
- Post-Sale.

For each stage in the buying cycle, we suggest selling actions that may be appropriate, and we note the **SELECT SELLING** tools that you should use (see **Figure 18**).

Requirements

Your customers either understand their requirements, or they need to be educated as to their need to change. This is often dependent on the stage of market maturity for your product or service offering. Understanding the requirement will give impetus to change and lead the customer to seek out potential solutions, assessing options and the potential benefit to be gained. This stage is the best opportunity you have to shape the need, develop the requirements, and guide the customer along your chosen path, assuming that you can show potential business benefit to be gained from purchasing your solution.

Evidence

The customer is now engaged in the evaluation process, gathering data and evidence that your solution can satisfy their requirements. At this stage in the process, there may be a little further development of the requirements, but the customer is primarily focused on whether a solution exists to deliver the benefits he wants. He needs to be comfortable with you, your company and your product. He will now be concerned, consciously or sub-consciously, with how he will justify his decision subsequently, either to be confident for himself that he has made the right choice, or to explain to other people within the company that the evaluation was thorough and fair.

Acquisition

In the eyes of the customer, this is the time of highest risk and you must act accordingly. The customer has gathered the data on each of the potential solutions and now needs to make a choice. To proceed or not to proceed – that is the question. He will be worried about making the right decision and will expend considerable resource looking at how to mitigate risk. By selecting one vendor, he will likely be committing to a long-term relationship. Hopefully, at this stage, you will have managed to assuage his fears and will have established a level of trust. Now the negotiators will be rolled in and focus will shift from value to cost.

Post-Sale

Congratulations. You got the deal. But it's not over. This should be the start of a long-term, mutually profitable relationship. It was hard work to get this far and it's going to be much easier to sell additional products or services to this customer, than it is to get another one. That is, if you take care of this customer. The most demoralizing thing in the world for a sales person is an unhappy or angry customer – and it's clearly not a good scenario for the customer.

Figure 18: The Buying Cycle – Selling Actions & Select Selling Tools

	Selling Actions	Select Selling Tools
Requirements	• Educate the customer on the benefit of change. • Understand the customer's pain and business impact of that pain. • Test his understanding of the benefits of change and his desire to invest in a solution. • Create value in the mind of the customer by articulating business benefit. • Focus the customer on the important aspects you want considered for evaluation. • Agree a buying cycle framework with checkpoints and mutual resource investment.	• Progressive Questioning Control Model • 4M Qualification Model • Pipeline Management Model
Evidence	• Show value through demonstrations and descriptions of other successful customers in their industry. • Show value through your understanding of the application of your offering to their business, contextualized for their particular company. • Highlight competitive advantage to be gained over their competition and demonstrate your competitive value over your competition. • Articulate benefits to be delivered by you, your company and your product and test their understanding of these benefits. • Work with the customer to understand the Return on Investment to be gained. • Establish any perceived risk to the budget, or to the project's momentum. • Understand the customer's perspective on your position relative to your competitor. Be aware of the value he perceives the competitor brings. • Confirm progress against the agreed buying cycle framework.	• Progressive Questioning Control Model • Power Gauge • Sales Planning Worksheet • 4M Qualification Model • Pipeline Management Model

	Selling Actions	SELECT SELLING Tools
Acquisition	• Understand the risks the customer perceives and articulate a risk plan to lessen those risks. • Restate your value. • Facilitate reference calls or visits with other customers. • Restate your commitment to partnership with the customer. • Restate competitive position. • Confirm progress against the agreed buying cycle framework.	• Negotiation Model • Power Gauge • Sales Planning Worksheet • 4M Qualification Model • Pipeline Management Model
Post-Sale	• Follow up with the customer to make certain his needs are being met and progress is as per expectation. • Co-ordinate resources within your organization to resolve issues quickly. • Maintain frequent communication with the customer to show your continued interest in his success. • Be honest about problems and engage, not in blame allocation, but in problem resolution. • Continue to develop your relationship with the customer for future mutual gain. • After the sale, when all is going well, ask for a referral.	

CONCLUSION

Today's buyer is a highly evolved professional. In most cases, he will have a detailed plan to procure products or services to meet a need. You too must have a plan and must implant yourself in his buying process as early as possible. That way you can influence its content and direction.

You must recognize and identify the six roles that are inherent in any complex purchase, understand the motivation for each of these functions, and ascertain how you can harness that motivation by adding value to each role. Marshall the resources you need. Use other departments or senior executives in your company to support your sales efforts. Use the SELECT SELLING Power Gauge to monitor your access to all the layers of power in the customer's company as they pertain to the particular sale, engage all of the parties during the cycle, and don't leave any of the influencers out in the cold.

Continually look at things from the other side of the table. Embrace the buyer's perspective; recognizing that there are four phases in the buying cycle. Tailor your selling activities accordingly, to achieve true alignment. When you look at things from the customer's viewpoint, you will see with uncommon clarity that you are both on a quest for the same thing – a profitable transaction that is mutually beneficial into the future.

CHAPTER SUMMARY: MEMO TO THE SALES SPECIALIST

- A typical buying process in a large corporation is complex. Your job is to be part of the process as early as you can.
- You must assume that the customer has a professional buying plan.
- Identify the six buying influencers.
- The **LOB Manager** has functional responsibility, general budget control, and is concerned with solving a particular business problem.
- The **User** is concerned about the day-to-day operational issues of using your product.
- The **Evaluator**'s focus will be technical. His concerns will include product features, and the fit of your solution with existing in-house infrastructure and expertise.
- Focus on ROI, and bottom line, for the **Financial Buyer**.
- Engage with the **Legal Buyer** early. Otherwise, he will see his role exclusively as protecting his company's interests, disregarding your value.
- The **Internal Champion** will guide the way. Ensure he has influence.
- Use the **SELECT SELLING** Power Gauge to monitor your access to the buying influencers.
- The buying cycle has four phases and the buyer's priorities change during each phase. The phase and priorities are: **Requirements** - Buyer Needs; **Evidence** - Proven Solution; **Acquisition** - Risk and Price; **Post-Sale** - Risk.

CHAPTER 5
DISCOVER, DEVELOP & CONTROL THE OPPORTUNITY

One of the biggest mistakes made by many technology companies is assuming that all customers are created equal. It's as if they expect some alchemist to stir a magic potion and to serve up cookie-cutter customers, each with the same level of technical savvy, common approach to risk, and similar awareness of their need. But, of course, it isn't so. While it's reasonable to expect that companies of like profile might make parallel purchases of similar products, the particular peculiarities of a buyer in one company may well dictate that he doesn't even know that he has a need – even when his counterpart in another company will have successfully completed the implementation and progressed to his next project. Customers are different – so why do so many sales professionals not spend enough time considering the context of the customer's viewpoint? We've said it before – but it's important, so we'll say it again: embrace the buyer's perspective. It's his money after all, and doing so will help you get it.

This chapter is about understanding what is going on inside the customer's head. Where does he want to go? Where's the origin of his journey? We want to guide him somewhere – so it makes sense to know where he is starting from.

This chapter is also about taking control of the sale. We start with the SELECT SELLING Progressive Questioning Control Model, or PQCM, to help you enhance your own questioning techniques within a structured framework.

Later in the chapter, we describe three customer types differentiated by their readiness to buy. Using PQCM, you will be able to assist each of these understand the potential benefits they might gain, by addressing the problem you help them uncover.

Questions, well crafted, help you to gain competitive advantage by having more information than your competitors, through the provoking of considered responses from your customer. If you can use that information to shape the development of his need, and be a guide for his journey, you can take control of the sale and increase dramatically your chance of success. In fact, you can decide to win!

THE SELECT SELLING PROGRESSIVE QUESTIONING CONTROL MODEL

It was Albert Einstein who said, "The important thing is to not stop questioning". Maybe Einstein didn't know it at the time, but he was in effect writing the first page of Sales 101, the beginner's sales lesson. Coupled with listening skills, proficiency in questioning techniques is one of the sales professional's most precious competencies. It helps you earn the right to get time from the customer to learn about his needs and pain.

Questions can be simple, eliciting factual responses, all the while provoking thought processes in the respondent. The questions you ask guide those thought processes:

- "When do you expect this project to start?"
- "How many people will participate?"

Other questions may hunt for explanation or elaboration, prompting the respondent to consider relative values (a good one for Einstein!):

- "Why would you start the project in May rather than June?"
- "Why would you fund this project rather than the other one?"

Good questions, well asked, show interest and can uncover a wealth of information. If you can engage your customer in supposition, hypothesis or conjecture, in a controlled manner, you can guide them to a deep understanding of the potential benefits of change:

- "Imagine if you could reduce your customer service response time by a third. How do you suppose that would impact the company?"

Wouldn't you rather if the customer came up with the ideas? Stimulate their creative juices and you might get valuable insights into the real issues that keep them up at night:

- "What do you think about the benefits of outsourcing some of your non-core activities? How do you think your employees will feel about it?"

Customers don't like being sold and recognize traditional techniques that try to push them to march to your agenda. Questions can be very powerful. Used well, they can uncover or develop a buying need for the customer, assist the customer navigate *your* chosen path, illuminating ways to look up alleys, to see which ones are blind. Use questions to guide – not push.

Have you ever been on the receiving end of one of those unsolicited hard-sell phone calls? You know the type.

> "Hi, Mr. Smith, would you like to be able to retire in your forties, having secured the future for yourself and you family?" Well, yes! "You have just been selected to participate in a limited offer to give you the chance to let you do just that. Would you like to know more?"

Although this technique is effective for many consumer products, it is not a tactic to use when partnering with a corporate customer for a complex technology sell.

A friend of ours recounts a tale of an insurance salesman with an unusual sales tactic. He would read the obituaries in the local paper and then target the neighborhood of the deceased. His pitch was:

> "It was sad to hear about Mrs. Jones who passed away last week. It was particularly unfortunate, as Mrs. Jones didn't sign the life assurance policy before her death. You don't want that to happen to you now, do you?"

These stories are extreme examples of coercive selling and neither passes the integrity test. Yet, they both speak to the power of the considered question – getting into the mind of the buyer, understanding his wants and fears and exploiting them.

The **SELECT SELLING** Progressive Questioning Control Model (see **Figure 19**) is not about exploitation of the customer, but is about exploiting the power of questioning, opening doors for the customer to peek through, uncovering possibilities hitherto unknown, and plotting a path for the customer to explore to discover potential benefit.

FIGURE 19: THE SELECT SELLING PROGRESSIVE QUESTIONING CONTROL MODEL

Question Type	Explore Cause	Determine Impact	Suggest Solution	Agree Action
Discover	1	4	7	10
Develop	2	5	8	11
Control	3	6	9	12

Time →

PQCM uses three different question types, each applied against the four stages of questioning progress:

- **Discover** questions should be open and inviting, giving the customer an opportunity to talk, prompting the customer to tell you about areas that are of concern to him.
- Once you have identified these areas of concern, you can progress to the **Develop** questions to expand your understanding of the extent of customer pain and to guide the customer to areas where your particular solution is strong.
- You close your questioning for each stage of question with **Control** questions to show the customer that you have been listening to what he says and that your understanding of his problem and perspective is correct.

You begin your diagnosis in the **Explore Cause** stage, working collaboratively with the customer, examining the reason and cause of his business pain, helping him articulate his customer's perspective. Once the pain and the cause of that pain is understood, you can move on to the **Determine Impact** stage seeking to uncover the customer's values, needs and motivations. When you get to **Suggest Solution**, you want to work with your customer to find a solution to his problem, figuring out what needs to be done and proffering potential alternatives. Finally, your goal is to get the customer to commit to a next step, using your questions in the **Agree Action** stage.

When you have used PQCM for a while, you will gain a fluency that will allow you to adopt it for different stages of the selling cycle. Before meetings, you can determine the information you are looking for, and the progress you want to make, and prepare your questions accordingly.

PQCM IN ACTION

At a recent conference, we presented to a group of CEOs of small technology companies. Most of the companies were less than a year old, and most of the CEOs had jumped from the comfort of a large corporation, to begin the tumultuous adventure of building their own business. We asked them to identify their greatest challenge. Apart from the usual difficult equation of balancing limited resources with unlimited tasks, one common concern emerged. It was well-articulated by George, one of the attendees, whose company had already secured a number of deals with a small number of large companies:

> "I provide machine visioning solutions to observe tasks that otherwise would have to be monitored by people, so cost savings are immediate (fewer people) and our machine makes fewer observation errors, so the manufacturing process is more efficient. My machine is like a virtual supervisor that's always on top of his game, eyes keen, always awake, seeing things that humans miss. However, my problem is sales. Right now, I'm the main sales guy – but I was always the customer in my previous company. I don't want to be the pushy, foot-in-the-door, pain-in-the-neck type. That's not me. When I was buying from suppliers in my previous role, many of the sales people became good friends of mine and we worked together to find the best way for my company to use their products. But many of the potential customers for my product don't know that a solution such as ours exists, so I have to expend a lot of time explaining it. When I get to do the demo, everyone gets really excited and it looks like we are going to get a deal, and then in many cases the project gets canned out of the blue. How can I get more control of this?"

On further exploration, George's problem touched on three main areas. The first was development of an unknown need. Getting access to all of the buying roles in the company was the main reason why projects were being 'canned out of the blue' (see **Chapter 4**). George was not getting to the Financial Buyer and couldn't figure out how to get there, and finally he wasn't controlling the sales cycle at all. These issues are common problems and can be alleviated by a structured and controlled questioning process.

We developed PQCM to solve this sort of problem (we address George's problem later in the chapter). It won't guarantee absolute success all of the time, but it will help you to demonstrate value to the customer, to identify winners (and losers) early and to put control of the sales cycle back in your hands.

Using PQCM

PQCM is a framework for you to use at each stage in the sales cycle to help you achieve five goals:

1. Explore with the customer the problem you propose to solve.
2. Determine the impact on his organization of not addressing the task.
3. Jointly visualize solutions and their attendant benefits.
4. Agree actions to take.
5. Plan each sales call or meeting.

We would not suggest that a framework such as this should be rigid or inflexible. But it should be fluid, only to the extent that the context of each conversation is different, revolving on the three axes of:

- Buyer awareness.
- Stage of the sales cycle
- The degree of discontinuity inherent in your product offering – in other words, will the customer have to make fundamental changes to his business if he adopts your product?

You will win more deals, more often, if you apply this model, work out the types of questions that are effective at each stage, and prepare well.

Having reached this point in the book (thanks for your perseverance!), you will be well-versed in the need for pain. Unless a customer has a problem to solve or pain to cure, there is no occasion to help, no justification for engagement, and no chance to develop a propitious opportunity. So, it makes sense to set off on our journey by understanding the problem or incipient pain, or highlighting the potential gains to be achieved by the customer.

In PQCM, we start at the beginning to explore the cause of the pain. We then figure out the impact of the problem, work towards a solution and agree an action plan. PQCM delineates between each of these phases, and as set out earlier, we describe them as:

- Explore Cause.
- Determine Impact.
- Suggest Solution
- Agree Action.

In chatting with George, we established that one major issue in his target market was the proximity of highly-sensitive components to one another, on the manufacturing line. We can use George's scenario from above as an example to see how we could apply the model to smooth out some of the bumps in the road.

FIGURE 20: USING PQCM – EXPLORE CAUSE

Explore Cause	Determine Impact	Suggest Solution	Agree Action
Either the customer understands he has a problem and is actively looking for a solution, or doesn't believe he has a problem or that a solution exists to solve it.			
Questions			
Discover	As the widgets are manufactured, how do you monitor the proximity of each new component to see that it's not too close to the previous one? Are there many staff doing that? Are there critical things they have to do? Do you have a 'normal' failure rate? Is this acceptable? Are there significant improvement possibilities? Is this a problem you are trying to solve?		
Develop	Are the inefficiencies as a result of poor training? Is it because it is just difficult for an operator to concentrate all the time?		
Control	So what you are saying is that the level of staff turnover is making it difficult to keep training levels up and, even for trained staff, it is hard to maintain concentration, so they don't catch all of the imperfections. Now you've been given the task of fixing this problem, but you don't know where to start. Have I got it right?		

What have we achieved so far? We understand now that the customer knows he has a problem. We have a sense as to where he sees the specific issues. Our **Discover** questions have given him the opportunity to focus on what he sees as being important. The **Develop** questions highlight for the customer some of the potential causes for his problem. Then to be sure that we listened well and heard correctly, we asked the customer to confirm our understanding of the situation.

For each problem area, the questions you use will be different. As we can't hear the customer's replies to our questions, this is an artificially contrived example, albeit based on a real set of circumstances. Stretch your mind now to think about how you might adapt this to your own situation. Start by listing the business problems that you think your solution solves. All you are trying to achieve at this stage of PQCM is to learn about the customer's awareness of need and to develop that need. Since George can solve the problem of poor training by replacing the operator with his machine, he is developing that opportunity in the mind of the customer. He is going to need to develop a more critical problem that he can solve – but that will come later.

Figure 21: Using PQCM – Determine Impact

Explore Cause	Determine Impact	Suggest Solution	Agree Action
You need to look beyond the obvious impact to consider how big a problem this really is for the customers and consequently how much value you can deliver.			
Questions			
Discover	What's the impact of releasing product with imperfections? Who is impacted? How is that manifested?		
Develop	Do your customers ever return product or hold up payment because of these problems? If these operators were re-deployed somewhere else, what impact would that have? Does this affect customer service costs? Do you know whether this is impacting on repeat business?		
Control	This seems like a significant problem – but also a significant cost savings opportunity. It seems to me that most departments are impacted here; finance, customer services, and operations. Is that right?		

We've uncovered some nuggets! The opportunity extends beyond a single department. To get full value for our solution, we will need to engage with each of the other departments. Getting access to multiple layers in the company will decrease the chance of unknown entities killing the project. We still don't know the buying process, but we are now entitled to ask for permission to talk to the others who are impacted. We also have the right to start asking about how a budget for this might be allocated and whether multiple departments are involved. This gives us insight into the project approval process and budgeting procedures. We are successfully developing the need and have identified an opportunity to create value, if we can solve the problem.

FIGURE 22: USING PQCM – SUGGEST SOLUTION

Explore Cause	Determine Impact	Suggest Solution	Agree Action
It's time to develop a joint solution vision with the customer and to create value by helping the customer to identify the best application of your type of product or service.			
Questions			
Discover	What's your ideal solution? What's most urgent for you? Are there specific elements of a solution that you must have quickly?		
Develop	What if you could identify glitches 100% of the time? Would it help if there were a way to automatically do the inspection?		
Control	So, you think that we would go a long way to solving the problem – cut down on product returns, free up operators, and improve your cash-flow by getting paid earlier – if you could apply technology that removes the human error element consistently. Have I got that right?		

If you understand the customer's business, you can add value. Throughout this process, you are embracing his perspective: helping him to visualize the potential benefits to be gained, and the application of your [type of] product or service to deliver those gains. Clearly, you need to determine how your product's benefits can be incorporated into this vision.

We have now identified, with the customer, a joint vision of the problem, the impact of the problem, and a way to overcome it. Next, we must agree a way forward.

FIGURE 23: USING PQCM – AGREE ACTION

Explore Cause	Determine Impact	Suggest Solution	Agree Action

Having created or developed the need, you need to guard against a competitor usurping your opportunity. Now you must get agreement to a joint way forward.	
Questions	
Discover	Where do we go from here? What's the usual process in the company for this kind of project? Who else do we need to involve? Is there anything else I need to know?
Develop	If I prepare a business impact study for your company, can we get all the people together to discuss? Would it be better if I got the CFO's input before or after that meeting? Can we agree a set of objectives to achieve over the next month to move this along? We're both going to be putting a lot of effort into this and we need to know if it's working.
Control	I will get the resources aligned to do the impact study and I'll draw up a list of the objectives we have agreed. If you can set up the meeting with the CFO and the group meeting to discuss the impact study, then it looks like we have a plan. Is all that ok with you?

Remember George's problem? We identified three areas that we looked to improve. The first was need development, the second was getting access to all of the buying roles in the company, and the third was controlling the sales cycle. Through the **Explore Cause** and **Determine Impact** phases of PQCM, George has a better chance now of developing and shaping the need for the customer. Coupling the **Agree Action** questions with **Determine Impact** helps him to 'get layered' in the organization, getting access to more influencers. And finally, combining the **Suggest Solution** phase with **Agree Action** questions gives him a platform to understand the buying process and to agree with the customer a framework by which he can control the sales cycle.

At each stage along the way, you must make sure that your understanding of the progress being made correlates with the customer's view. Offer to document the achievements along the way. Confirm decisions made by email after a meeting. Use written communication to record the information you have gathered and to ensure that the customer has the same understanding.

Applying PQCM

Questions are powerful. To leverage PQCM for your own scenario, you must do some work to list what questions might work with your customer. It should be clear that expertise in the customer's business is a necessity, and a singular focus on the industry you serve will deliver rewards. In **Figure 24**, we have set out generic question types that will help you select questions that can be applied. You need to focus on winners and work with customers who want to engage. Spend the time, figure out the questions and gain the benefits. However, don't forget that all customers are different, and that different questions will work for different stages in the buying cycle. PQCM is a living thing.

The SELECT SELLING Progressive Questioning Control Model template and sample questions are available to download at www.selectselling.com.

FIGURE 24: A GENERIC SELECT SELLING PROGRESSIVE QUESTIONING CONTROL MODEL

Question Type	Explore Cause	Determine Impact	Suggest Solution	Agree Action
Discover	What is the business problem?	Who is impacted?	How do you think we can fix it?	What is our first step?
Develop	Is it [possible area of problem]?	Does this impact on [business area]?	Suppose it was possible to ..	When would you like to .. ?
Control	So what you are saying is [restate the problem]	So [name] suffers and the [business area] too	If that's possible you think we could ..	If I deliver this will you ...?

Time →

CUSTOMERS ARE DIFFERENT

In 1991, Geoffrey Moore presented a refreshing perspective of the Technology Adoption Life Cycle, or TALC, in his seminal book, *Crossing the Chasm*. The proposition set out in the book is that customers can be segmented by their position on the TALC curve, and that the market determines whether a product or technology is emerging or mature. According to Moore, customers can be described as visionaries, pragmatists, conservatives or skeptics, and each will exhibit a different degree of receptivity to new ideas and products. Some, the visionaries, will be aware of the possibilities afforded by a technological solution as soon as the technology is introduced to the market. Others, the pragmatists, will wait a while for the market to mature a little and won't be willing to take the lead until the technology has proved itself somewhat. In many cases, they can see the possibilities of the solution but don't necessarily know how to apply it to their particular circumstance. Conservatives will wait for the technology to be truly established before embarking on an implementation. Frequently, they too require help to determine how the application of the technology will help their business. Finally, the skeptics will wait until everyone else has jumped on board first and the technology becomes commoditized – and then they're primarily concerned with price.

The core differentiator between Moore's four groups is their willingness to change or, more fundamentally, their awareness of their need, the problem they have to solve, or the potential gains to be had. Without change, there is no opportunity for you or your competitors. If the awareness of need isn't there, the value you can offer is irrelevant. If they don't think they have a problem, then from their perspective – and that's the only one that counts – you don't have a solution. It's not a solution, unless the customer thinks it is. If you don't have a solution, then you certainly can't make the sale. Just because you think that they should want to change, to adopt a solution such as yours, doesn't mean that they will.

So, what do you do about it? Well, to start, you need to understand where they are coming from. You need to assess the situation. You must accept that different customers have different levels of need awareness. The more they understand that they have a problem, the more likely they are to buy something to fix it. The customer's awareness of need can be correlated directly with your map of their buying cycle. If they know they have a problem, then they will buy something from somebody to solve it. If not, you have a bit to go before they even resemble a qualified prospect.

Your challenge is two-fold. First, you need to identify the intensity of resistance to change. Are they aware of the need? Then, once you have a fix on the customer's perspective, you must figure out what to do about it. How can you sell the same product to different customers, if they have different levels of need awareness?

At a high level, this problem can be addressed though effective strategic positioning and clear articulation of the value delivered by products such as yours (see **Chapter 3**). There remains, however, the practical, one-on-one, real-life scenario when you are sitting across from a customer who, in your mind, *'just doesn't get it'*. How do you educate, encourage, or convince a customer who doesn't see the need to change or can't visualize the benefits that might accrue?

THREE TYPES OF CUSTOMER NEED

Having interacted with many buyers, researched existing material, and interviewed a number of sales professionals, it is evident to us that strong patterns exist that correlate a buyer's level of need awareness directly with his propensity to buy something from somebody, and inversely with your opportunity to create value.

The three types of customer need (see **Figure 25**) are:

- Unknown.
- Known.
- Active.

Those who have an Unknown need are most in need of your help and therefore more receptive to value creation, while those in the Active camp are most likely to buy something soon. Each of these customer types needs to be dealt with differently.

FIGURE 25: THE THREE TYPES OF CUSTOMER NEED

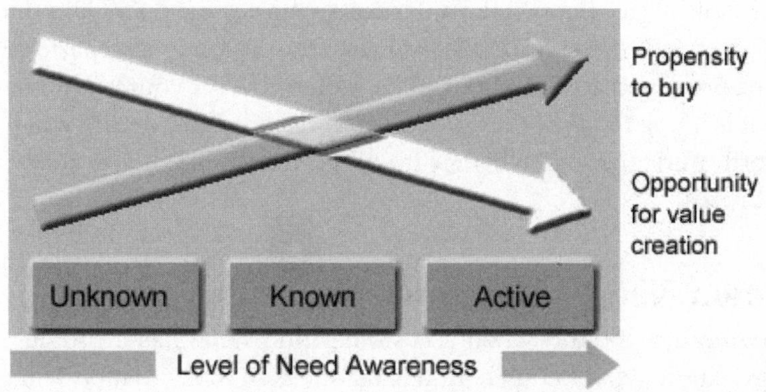

Unknown Need – Unknown Problem

Even though your product might be flush with competitive features, each designed meticulously to deliver real business value, the customer might not care. That's his prerogative! If the customer does not feel business pain, or does not believe that his problem can be solved, or considers that the attendant risks in addressing the problem are too high, then he doesn't see why he should take it on. He can't visualize a reason to change.

Assuming that your product or service offering in fact would deliver benefit to this customer, then something is amiss. We call this an Unknown Need. The need is there, but the customer has not yet realized it and, from the salesperson's perspective, this is a hard situation to develop. If you are selling an emerging product or technology, it is likely that the marketplace will place your offering early in the Technology Adoption Life Cycle, and it is likely that you will find customers with Unknown Needs.

As of yet, the customer has not accepted that your solution is important to him and will classify it as 'a solution looking for a problem'. He is certainly not engaged in trying to find a solution, because either he is satisfied with the way he currently manages his situation, or just doesn't believe that a viable solution exists. When a customer's awareness of need is unknown, the cost of sale is very high, the sales cycle is long, and you must place education, 'success stories' and case studies at the top of your agenda as you wait for the penny to drop.

Assuming that you have targeted the customer correctly, it's worth maintaining frequent contact and developing the relationship in order to be recognized as the solution source when the customer comes around. Educate the customer on the changing trends in his industry. Communicate as many relevant success stories as possible – but be careful to focus on the direct relevance to the customer's scenario or you will be perceived as wasting his time. Determine for yourself how much time it is going to take to develop the opportunity and decide whether it is worth pursuing and whether it will be worth winning in the end. If not, drop it.

Known Need – Unknown Solution

Opportunities abound when a customer knows he has a problem but doesn't know what to do about it. Customers in that situation will place high value on consultative support to aid in the development of a strategic buying vision. They will take comfort from your experience of similar situations with their counterparts in other companies and will value your experience. They will place great value on your ability to identify for them opportunities for application of your product or service that add value to their business. Going beyond obvious product features, or obvious applications, the customer will want you to help them uncover business process improvements that you can help them achieve.

Anxiety levels are high and the customer feels at risk because he can't necessarily visualize the solution. If you can transcend the vendor perspective and be more than 'just a provider', the customer will go the extra mile for you. He will also be less focused on squeezing your margins, if you join with him in establishing a long-term joint vendor/customer vision.

Active Need – Solution Vision

When senior executives move from one organization to another in their industry, they will often be charged with using the experience gained in their previous company to accelerate the deployment of new systems at their new location. As a buyer, or a prospective customer, this executive will be typical of a customer with an Active need; he will actively want to work with a supplier (not necessarily the same one as before) to determine quickly the actions to be taken to implement a solution to solve the known problem. He undoubtedly has a vision of the possible solution and understands that it's his responsibility to get the job done.

Without doubt, this is a qualified sales opportunity, and the buying cycle should be shorter than in either of the other two scenarios above. However, the bar is set a little higher and it will be somewhat more difficult for you to add value in the application of your product to establish creative solutions, as the customer is already quite proficient, and might well achieve the solution unaided. You need to focus not just on the 'what', but also the 'how'. The customer knows what he wants. You need to be able to identify for him how to best apply the product, how you can help better than anyone else, and how you have that 'special idea' that will add extra value.

CONCLUSION

Your innate ability to reason is only fully exercised by a developed ability to question. For each of our customer types (Unknown Need, Known Need, and Active Need), persistent questioning will deepen your perception of the real issues particular to that customer, or the hot buttons he truly cares about. The **SELECT SELLING Progressive Questioning Control Model** is a methodology that we have seen used very effectively. Using well-crafted questions, we have seen Sales Specialists achieve an uncommon comprehension of the view from the other side of the table. This approach will accelerate your ability to embrace the buyer's perspective and then discover, develop and control the opportunity.

CHAPTER SUMMARY: MEMO TO THE SALES SPECIALIST

- Customers are different. You need to understand their individual perspective.
- The **SELECT SELLING Progressive Questioning Control Model** will help you to: explore the customer's problem; determine the impact of the problem; visualize a solution with the customer, and agree actions.
- **Discover** questions invite the customer to explain his business need.
- **Develop** questions expand your understanding of the problem.
- **Control** questions confirm your understanding, and the customer's commitment.
- There are three type of customer need: Unknown, Known and Active.
- Customers with an **Unknown** need are receptive to value creation, but are unlikely to buy soon.
- You can develop value for customers with a **Known** need, and guide them to purchase in a fairly short time.
- Customers with an **Active** need have the greatest propensity to buy quickly.

CHAPTER 6

DO YOU QUALIFY TO SELL?

What is the greatest source of fairy tales? Is it Walt Disney, the Brothers Grimm or Hans Christian Andersen? Or maybe it's buyers. Dare we suggest that it might be salespeople?

What's the difference between a story from Hans Christian Andersen and a poorly qualified forecasted sale? One's a fairy tale with a happy ending. The other, well that's more 'grim' than Grimm (sorry!).

A good friend and client of ours is a senior sales executive with a technology company. His company provides Internet security products to large corporations. Mike has responsibility for a large sales team spread across the country. Every Friday morning, he has a meeting with his sales team to review progress. You know the usual:

- "What's your pipeline looking like?"
- "What can I do to help you finalize the deal?"
- "Are you ready to forecast that opportunity to close in this quarter?"

Mike is well-liked by his sales team. He always steps up to the plate to get things done, if something is hurting either the customer or the sale. He has helped the team implement SELECT SELLING, getting budget approval in tight times. His investment and belief is now paying off for him and his company, and his sales team is getting bigger commission checks. Mike's always available for sales calls and will go out of his way for any of his team and will work the company internal structure to get issues resolved.

He asks for only one thing in return – accurate forecasts. Mike has a favorite saying, which seems strange at first but it's one with which his team is very familiar:

> "Two is not equal to three, not even for large values of two."

It's another way of saying: it is what it is, or: if it looks like a duck, walks like a duck, and quacks like a duck, then it's a duck. In short, if a deal is not well qualified, then don't pretend that it is and don't forecast it.

Mike is a stickler for sales process in general, but qualification in particular:

> "Why work on unqualified opportunities when you could be making money?"

He runs a great sales organization, manages to minimize 'quarter-end crunch' most of the time, and is remarkably accurate with the forecasts for his team, month after month, quarter after quarter. Mike knows his business and manages it well, through effective qualification.

Effective qualification, as an integral part of the sales process, is a supremely valuable tool, not just for the sales organization, but for the company overall. Link precise qualification with your sales process stages and your pipeline management, and then you know what's going on! Depending on the questions you ask and the information you glean, you can determine how likely the sale is to close:

- Has the customer an identified project?
- Is budget allocated?
- Do you know the compelling event that will motivate the customer to buy?
- Are all of the influencers identified?
- What roles do they play?
- Have you won this type of business before?
- Can you win this one?
- What's your source of information?
- Are there any competing projects?
- Do you fully understand the buyer's needs?
- Can you meet them competitively?

Unless you have a crystal ball, you cannot forecast accurately if you don't qualify properly. Poor qualification leads to missed numbers and surprise sales losses. If internal resources are allocated based on your pipeline, your credibility is seriously damaged, and your customers will slip down the priority list when internal resources are getting allocated.

> We spoke to a client of ours on June 29, 2004. His sales team's revenue goal for the quarter was $12 million, and he called us for help. They were $1 million short, had one day left in the quarter, and one of the sales team had a verbal order for $2 million. Normally, the finance department would give a little leeway at the end of the quarter. They usually would have let the sales team recognize the verbal order as long as the paperwork was following soon. In this case, the CFO just didn't believe the sales person, because all her forecasts in the past were wrong. It turns out that the deal was solid, but they missed the quarter number just because the credibility of the sales person was shot – based on a history of bad forecasting, born of poor qualification. We couldn't do anything to help.

There's a lesson here for the sales person, sales management and the CEO. You can't have senior managers going on every sales call or checking up on the status of the sale, just in order to forecast it. But an agreed set of qualification checkpoints that map to various stages in the sales pipeline reduces the management overhead, introduces a common language, cuts down on forecasting errors or uncertainties, and let's the sales person get on with the job – according to the rules.

THE QUALIFICATION PROCESS

Good qualification methods help you weed out losers early. It's better to have a few holes in your pipeline that you can identify, rather than kid yourself with a pipeline bulging with puffed-up no-hopers. With effective qualification (using the **SELECT SELLING** Progressive Questioning Control Model), you uncover information to sharpen your focus on the deals that are worth winning. You become proficient in spotting upcoming obstacles in time to prepare. Sales Specialists will qualify relentlessly, using the qualification process as a platform to build mutual respect and deep relationships with their customers. They continuously exceed their goals. Wishful Thinkers don't qualify well, maintain huge pipelines – and close few deals. They get fired frequently.

Qualification is not an event. It's an ongoing process. As buyers evaluate you, you must continue to qualify them. If you are a 'value creator' during the evaluation, you've earned the right to probe deeper into the opportunity. Part of the qualification process involves establishing the rules of engagement and laying the groundwork for control of the sales process. You must make sure that you question for objective and accurate answers. Ask the same question of different influencers in the account, and you will be surprised at what you learn about the perspective of each role. You need to check that you're working on a real live opportunity. As Mike says, why work on unqualified opportunities when you could be making money?

One of the main benefits accruing from disciplined qualification is a pipeline that's credible and a forecast you can stand over – and deliver:

- When does a target become a qualified prospect that warrants extensive sales effort?
- How many qualified prospects do you need at each stage of the pipeline to meet your quota?
- Which qualifiers determine whether a deal is likely to close?
- How can you accurately predict the timing of a promised order?
- As you are getting to that final negotiation stage, what's the impact of poor qualification on your ability to strike a good deal?

If you use the structured qualification process we outline in this chapter, you will find that it helps you to uncover missing information or to prompt your next action. If adopted in your organization, it enhances productivity by having a common language throughout. Forecasts and pipelines become believable. What percentage of the deals you forecasted last year closed on schedule? We are confident that a better qualification system would have helped to provide an early warning system to strengthen the accuracy of your predictions.

So, which deals do you want to work on? Where's the threshold? In our view, you should be using qualification techniques to select opportunities that you have a better than 50% chance of winning. Then you can eliminate the rest and work with confidence to win your chosen few deals. And that's often the crux. It's not easy to walk away from opportunities – particularly the really big ones, even if you know in your gut that you don't have a hope of winning.

Should you respond to all sales opportunities with equal vigor? Clearly not! Sometimes you just have to say "No". If you don't think you can win, give up early and don't waste your time. When you select your customer well, embrace the buyer's perspective, and use a well-defined qualification process to express your value, you can decide which deals you want to win. This leads to productive focus, a higher conversion rate than normal, and accurate sales forecasts.

LISTEN AS YOU QUALIFY

As you will have learnt from the Progressive Questioning Control Model, we place a lot of store in the value of questions. Often, you can find yourself so anxious to get your message across that you spend all of your time telling the customer about what you have, rather than exploring his perspective. When this happens, you are either speaking, or waiting to say the next thing, never listening properly. Listening, and listening well, will make your questioning more palatable for the customer and will result in more effective qualification.

When you ask a question, you should pause and wait for the customer to respond. To ensure you heard correctly, summarize what he said, and ask for confirmation that your interpretation is correct. Use the knowledge you gain to explore his needs and motivations. Listen actively to discover his true fears and concerns. As you listen, you should maintain eye contact with the customer, focusing on what he is saying and how he is saying it. Try to remove your emotions from your listening so that you hear what is actually being said, rather than what you want to hear. Your rate of thought will likely outpace his rate of speech and you should use that gap to consider what key points the customer is making. You have the ability to listen, think and consider at the same time, and all these should be focused on ensuring that you understand what the customer is saying. Before you respond, make sure he has said all he has to say. That way, your response can be complete and considered. Here's a true story.

Robin is five years old. Last year, just before Christmas, she came home from school and handed her father a note from her teacher. On reading the note, Robin's father was proud and excited. His daughter was going to be in the school Nativity play. OK, she's just five, and it was only a school play, but that's the way fathers get about their daughters. What Robin's Dad couldn't understand, however, was that she didn't seem at all pleased, which was unusual for Robin. Like most little girls, Robin loved playacting, dressing up and being on stage, especially if the dressing up involved wearing something pink!

"So, Robin", said her father, "aren't you pleased and thrilled to be in the play?"

"Yes, but I'm a shepherd", she replied.

"But that's great", he said enthusiastically, planning the home movie spectacular he would be recording of his little princess. "How were you picked to be a shepherd?"

> Robin offered her explanation. "Miss Williams told us that we were very lucky, our class was the only one that was allowed to have a play for Christmas. Then she asked who wanted to be a shepherd on the stage, and I put my hand up."
>
> She paused, turned to her father, "But how was I supposed to know there was going to be angels?"

Robin's clearly not a Sales Specialist. She didn't consider all the options before jumping in, and she didn't really listen well – but then, she's only five. We all have opportunities every day for deep listening, and we frequently squander these chances.

The Select Selling 4M Qualification Model

The **Select Selling 4M Qualification Model** (**Figure 26**), or 4MQ, is a structured process you can draw on to guide your interaction with the customer. 4MQ acts as a guide to help you identify information gaps and potential areas of risk and to align your selling activities to the customer's buying motion.

Figure 26: The Select Selling 4M Qualification Model

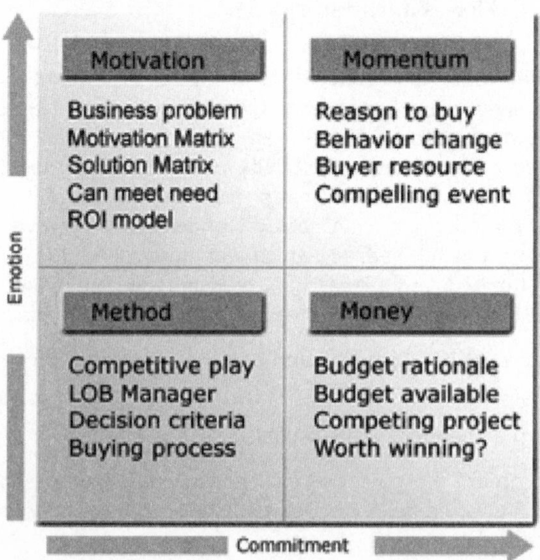

At all stages in the cycle, you should be trying to recognize the emotional dynamics at play, as well as driving to increase the buyer's commitment to a purchase.

4MQ segments qualification criteria into four categories:

- Method.
- Money.
- Motivation.
- Momentum.

As you investigate the buyer's method, you will learn about the buying and decision-making processes. Money is at the heart of any buying decision at some point in the cycle. Can the customer afford to buy and can you make money on the deal? You must be able to see the budget and determine whether there are any competing projects that might usurp the funding for your project.

If Money and Method are the 'how' of a purchase, Motivation is the 'why'. Motivation combines both personal and company reasons to invest in a solution such as yours. It's been said that the greatest competitor at any time is 'No Decision Inc'. Having evaluated many products or solutions, buyers will sometimes just not make any decision – at all! Unless you understand the Momentum that is driving the buyer to purchase and implement a solution, the opportunity isn't properly qualified, and you can be left with one of those deals that you forecast quarter after quarter, but never manage to get over the finishing line.

The 4MQ model and related qualification questions are summarized in **Figure 29**, at the end of the chapter.

4M Qualification: Method

What's the buying process?

You may recall, from **Chapter 4, Figure 13**, that the buying process in large corporations is increasingly becoming both disciplined and complex. The complexity and rigor of that process needs to be understood. What are the steps and tasks that the buyer has to complete in the buying process? Exploring with the buyer how they normally run a purchase project will illuminate many of the issues you need to know. If you are not already on the corporation's approved vendor list, you must determine whether that is a requirement for the buyer.

Who are the competitors?

If you have selected your customers correctly, with the rigor and discipline that we continually urge, you should win deals because you have a competitive advantage over other players. The customers you are dealing with are the ones that you have selected, based on the fit of your solution to their needs. If your competitors are equally disciplined, you should meet the same competitors frequently. If Siebel and salesforce.com are competing for the same business, then it's almost certain that one of them shouldn't be there. If you find that there are unusual competitors at the table in a particular opportunity, then you must ask yourself who lost their way. One of you is probably chasing the wrong deal.

Having knowledge of the competition for the sale is a key qualifier. Not only does it prepare you for comparative evaluation, but it also elucidates the buyer's frame of reference. It helps you get inside the buyer's mind and see the profile of supplier that they think might be able to solve their problem. If you can find out who the competitors are, you can look for the opportunity to ask the buyer what they value about your competitors, and how they plan to evaluate one vendor against another.

We would never encourage you to denigrate your competition and the buyer doesn't want you to do that either. It makes him look foolish for inviting them to bid for the business in the first place. However, if you can determine the value that the buyer perceives the competitor offers, you have learned about a benefit or feature that the buyer values. You can respond accordingly. Many times, we have seen deals lost because the competitor highlighted a specific benefit that the customer was really excited about, but the salesperson never knew. Because the salesperson didn't see that hot button, or saw the button but didn't recognize it was hot, he could not show how his company would address the issue or demonstrate how similar or greater benefit could be derived from their solution. You need to be prepared to articulate the competitive advantage offered by your solution over each of your key competitors. Then, if you know who the competitor is, for a given opportunity, you are better equipped to win.

Who is the LOB Manager?

Back in **Chapter 4**, we spelt out the multiple buying roles involved in a complex purchase. As you start to qualify a particular opportunity, you must understand early the business impact of the purchase, from the buyer's perspective. Bidding for business is a costly exercise. According to the Gartner Group, the average cost of a face-to-face sales call from a salesperson in the high-technology sector is more than $400. Combine that with the fact that win rates for deals where companies respond to unsolicited Request for Proposals (RFP) are typically less than 5%. And what's the cost of an RFP response? It varies from company to company but is certainly north of 15 working days for most complex sales. The need for early, solid qualification is clear.

One technology company had such a significant problem with conversion rates for sales opportunities that they asked us to review their bidding process. Because this company was very large, and had a widely-recognized brand, they always made it onto buyer's lists of potential vendors. The sales, marketing and services departments in the company spent a large proportion of their time bidding for business that they subsequently lost.

As we reviewed the opportunities they were pursuing, it became clear that they never said "No" when any potential sale reared its head. Apart from the fact that they were not assessing opportunities based on the fitness of their solution to the buyer's need, they clearly didn't have any steps in place to qualify the customer. They had no way of telling whether the RFP was just an exercise for the buyer in information-gathering, a request for competitive quotations to put pressure on an incumbent supplier or a standard operating procedure for the buyer's organization to have multiple proposals.

We asked Sam, the Vice President of Sales, to have another look at whether they should respond to all bid requests. With some further discussion and impact analysis, we quickly implemented a policy for the sales team to limit the number of bids they could pursue. We wanted them to work on deals they had a fair chance of winning.

Before the sales team could request support from the marketing or services departments to prepare a pitch, the salesperson had to speak with the buyer's LOB Manager to understand the business scenario that led them to start the buying cycle. In that call, we asked the salesperson to indicate the effort that he was going to undertake to create value for the buyer as part of the proposal. Of course, this would require substantial resource commitment.

Before the sales person could engage with the marketing and service team, he needed a written communication (most often, email) from the LOB Manager in the buyer's organization, confirming that if our client undertook to prepare a tailored proposal, customized for the buyer, that he would make sure that the our client had access to the relevant people in his company who our client might need to talk to in order to create the best possible proposal. The impact of this was gratifying.

First, the sales team objected. Of course, they weren't necessarily concerned with the cost of the bid process, since their compensation plan was focused on top line revenue only. We outlined for them how a more focused approach would be in the customer's interest, and set out how they could articulate the benefits of this approach to the customer. We also explained how we expected this to result in an increase in sales, and most of them got on board.

Next, some of the prospects declined to participate under these rules of engagement. However, with some encouragement, Sam held his line. As the sales team engaged the LOB Manager early in the buying cycle, they began to learn a lot about the opportunity. Some of the prospects turned out to be information-gatherers only, and Sam's team politely declined the invitation to participate. In the end, the number of formal bids was reduced by just more than half, cutting down our client's cost of sale.

Then an interesting thing happened. The buyers welcomed early engagement, seeing this process as an indication that our client was really interested in their business problem, and wanted to think about solving it rather than taking a cookie-cutter approach. The conversion rate increased nearly five-fold, resulting in a doubling of sales revenue for a reduced cost.

Sam's team benefited from a number of changes to their bid process. Although there were other factors that impacted, he is convinced that introducing this LOB Manager milestone was the main catalyst for his increased revenue. Whether this exact approach can work for your company, you must qualify the opportunity by having meaningful engagement with the LOB Manager early in his buying cycle.

What are the decision criteria?

How is the buyer going to choose a vendor? What are the key attributes he is looking for in his future business partner? What are his hot buttons? If you don't know the answer to these questions, you are unlikely to win the business. It is likely that the buyer's organization has developed a scorecard-type approach to vendor evaluation. This is almost certainly the case for very large projects or for government business. You need to know the headings on the scorecard and the weightings for each. In most cases, you will need to satisfy various criteria for your product or service offering. But you may also have to satisfy the buyer of your company's financial stability, your company's vision, your understanding of his business, your track record with your existing customers, or the view of industry analysts.

Who created the decision-making criteria? Who created the evaluation plan? If you weren't involved in the determination of the criteria, you need to make sure that your competitor didn't draw up the list. If you're a big company, has the customer any concerns about flexibility? If you're small, does he want you to partner with a big company to assist in the delivery? Perhaps there are specific criteria he will look at, involving product delivery or payment options.

It is rarely the case that buyers evaluate vendors on product features alone. You must understand each criterion so that you can put your best foot forward.

4M Qualification: Money

Show me the money!

Your reason for being in business is to extract money from a customer in exchange for a valuable product or service that you deliver. It's the basic equation of successful sales. You must be able to show the customer that your product will provide a financial return, based on increased value or decreased costs. In exchange, the customer must have the budget to pay for that product. Unless the customer has a Known or Active need (see **Chapter 5**), it is unlikely that he has an allocated budget. If he has an allocated budget, he probably understands his need to change and you are dealing with a real opportunity. Budgets are generally set at the start of a financial period by the CFO or CEO of a company and discretion is given to the function heads to spend the money. Sometimes, the allocation of those budgets is flexible, and other times less so. If you can show value creation to a sufficiently powerful buyer, then he can often find hitherto unavailable budgets to fund your project. Unless you have evidence that there is money available, and it is allocated to your project, you shouldn't treat this customer as a qualified opportunity.

What project is at the top of the totem pole?

Do you often think about why a customer has chosen this particular time to begin his buying cycle? Perhaps it's because you have invested time in educating him on the potential gains to be had. Maybe the CEO read an article in a business magazine that related the benefits achieved by a competitor. It could be the result of a company strategic off-site meeting, identifying quarterly or annual goals. Whatever the reason is, you can be sure that buying your product isn't the only thing your buyer is worrying about. It's not the only project they have to fund. You need to understand your position on the totem pole. If you're not at the top today, you might never get there, and you need to figure that out.

One of our favorite tactics that we advise our clients to use to determine the urgency of a purchase is to ask a simple question:

- "Why would you do Project A (our project) first, rather than Project B or C?"

Hopefully, the prospect's answer indicates that Project A is both important and urgent. If not, the prospect has to have sufficient budget for the other two projects, as well as the unexpected one that is sure to arise at some point. An opportunity needs to be both important and urgent for the buyer, for you to be sure that it won't slip. You need to understand what other projects are competing for 'your' budget. Only then can you categorize the opportunity as a qualified prospect that you may be able to forecast.

Where did he get the number?

If a customer says he has an approved project with allocated and authorized budget, many salespeople will get all excited and start forecasting the opportunity. But where did the customer get the number to put into his budget? If this is the first time you have heard about the opportunity, you need to determine which of your competitors helped him arrive at his estimate. It would be unusual for a buyer to submit a budget request, without at least talking to a potential supplier to assess the likely costs. If you are not that supplier, you're immediately at a disadvantage. What else do you think your competitor did when he helped the customer determine the budget? He probably helped him identify his goals for the project. He certainly has the edge in figuring out what the buyer really wants, and he is certainly at the top of the vendor list. You may well be just the second vendor that the buyer needs to submit to procurement, in line with company policy.

Can you afford to pursue it?

How does the profile of the deal impact your ability to deliver a profitable sale for your company? In a software product-based business, a deal that is worth $50,000 probably costs as much to close as one worth two or three times that amount. Profit levels are dramatically different in the two deals. You will have gone through the same proposal exercise, probably made the same number of presentations and sales calls, utilized the same technical support resource and racked up similar travel expenses. That's factor number one in determining the right profile of opportunities to pursue. They have to be of appropriate magnitude to reward you for your cost of sale. But, as you pursue larger deals, you need to make sure that they really are larger deals. Experienced buyers will frequently negotiate volume-pricing deals while giving volume purchase *indications,* not volume purchase *commitments.* Prices based on million-dollar volume purchase intentions don't pay for the cost of support, if the actual purchases are a fraction of the indicated volume.

Once you understand the buying process, and the buyer's buying cycle, you should be able to determine the resources that it will take for you to maintain a sustained effort right up to the end. This is one example where quitters do win. You should assess the effort that you know you will spend, perform your own risk analysis, judge the potential return that you hope you will get and decide whether it's worth participating. This advice is particularly appropriate for small companies dealing with larger ones. The big company has people whose job it is to manage a complex buying process. That's what they get paid to do. When small companies engage in this cycle, they really need to be sure that the opportunity is well-qualified, as the process will suck up all the resources that they can allocate.

One of the problems with committing a lot of resources to one opportunity – which you are inclined to do to 'win the big one' – is that, in most cases, it gets increasingly hard to quit. What do you do when it's late in the cycle and the buyer demands unreasonable service level commitments, looks for laughable indemnity provisions, or squeezes your margins until there's little left, or states that it's his company's policy not to pay maintenance in the first year? The salesperson, who sees this first, should decide to walk away if they can't negotiate better terms. But too frequently, he doesn't. Back at headquarters, people are counting on the deal. They are also measuring the amount of resource committed so far and understandably want some return. This is only human nature, but you have to accept that the resource committed already is gone and the commercial decision you are making will impact your profitability going forward. And that's not only for this customer. What happens when the customer debriefs the competitor who came in second? The next time he loses a deal to you, he may well be inclined to advise the other customer of the deal that you did this time and then it becomes a vicious circle.

4M Qualification: Motivation

Where's the personal why?

At first glance, the reason behind a buyer's decision to purchase a particular solution from a specific vendor may seem obvious, but people buy for many different reasons. Personal buying reasons have to do with emotional reasons, while corporate buying decisions are generally based on value. If the buyer personally dislikes interacting with the individual representing the vendor, he will very rarely buy from that vendor. Buyers want to be helped, and want to develop a trusted relationship with the vendor who can help them. That's the person they like to buy from. They value demonstrated honesty, integrity and competence.

The buyer who wants to be seen as an instrument of change in his company will choose to sign with the vendor who can help him achieve that. If you can help your buyer design the right solution for his company, and then help him deliver it, he will receive credit for identifying a good partner to work with, as well as being lauded for a successful implementation. Powerful buyers have strong personal track records and they don't want you to screw it up for them.

When projects fail, companies don't take the fall, people do. When projects succeed, recognition is bestowed on the project sponsors. What does the buyer have riding on this project? What does it mean to him if it succeeds/fails? It's necessary to understand the personal pain felt by each of your buying influencers and to craft a plan to cure that pain.

Personal pain will not necessarily be the same as the corporate business objective. Personal motivation rarely focuses on getting the absolute best price, but more on guaranteeing a successful completion. That's why we have seen some venture capitalists trumpet a sale of one of their portfolio companies, even when the (undisclosed) disposal price is less than their investment. It's not in their interest to be seen to have a failed investment. It's not good for their reputation.

No corporate pain, no business gain

Your task is to create and present a solution to solve your customer's problems, once you know what those problems are. In **Chapter 5**, we discussed Unknown, Known and Active Needs. Is the customer aware of the need? You must classify each potential opportunity as Unknown, Known or Active customer types. Unless the buyer knows that he has a need, you cannot call this a qualified opportunity. If there is a Known or

Active need, you must be able to clearly document it, describe his business pain, and the commercial impact of the problem.

Don't assume that you know best. Traditional sales people frequently offend potential buyers by trying to enforce their proposed solution without letting the buyer work his way through the problem. Often, it might be the case that you indeed know what's best. If you are a Sales Specialist, focused on one industry niche, running through the same problems with multiple customers on a daily basis, you should be able to see the solution sooner than your customer. But it's not a solution, unless the customer says that it is. He must envision how your product will be used to fix his problem. You probably understand how it is going to work, but whatever about understanding your product or his business problem better than he does, unless you are telepathic, you can't see what is going on in his mind. Let him get there in his own time, so that you have a deeply ingrained path to success carved in his mind. That way, you get to have a clearly articulated common vision that you can work on together to solve. Complete the **SELECT SELLING Motivation Matrix** (**Figure 27**) to test that you can describe the problem for each of the buying influencers.

FIGURE 27: THE SELECT SELLING MOTIVATION MATRIX

Buyer	Motivation & Pain
LOB Manager	
User Buyer	
Evaluator	
Financial	
Legal / Procurement	
Internal Champion	

Can we solve the problem?

You know the problem, the pain of the corporation and the personal motivation for each of the buying influencers. Assuming that you have selected the customer according to your guideline rules, you should be able to solve the problem, better than your competitors. If that is true, and the other qualifiers stack up, then you should have a good chance of winning the business, and you must feel comfortable about forecasting the deal. Use your Target Customer Selection rules to confirm that the customer meets your 'sweet spot' criteria, and then complete the **SELECT SELLING Solution Matrix (Figure 28)** to prove that you can solve the problem for each of the buyers.

FIGURE 28: THE SELECT SELLING SOLUTION MATRIX

Buyer	Solution
LOB Manager	
User Buyer	
Evaluator	
Financial	
Legal / Procurement	
Internal Champion	

What's the Return on Investment?

The customer is employed to serve his stakeholders: customers, employees, shareholders and community. He should only make an investment, if it serves one or more of those constituencies. Consequently, his centers of attention need to be productivity, profitability, cost efficiencies, regulatory compliance, revenue growth, improved customer satisfaction, increased quality, and the like.

As your customer decides to make an investment, you must help him determine what return he will get. For every dollar spent, there must be more than a dollar returned. That return can be measured in competitive advantage, increased brand, happier employees, conciliatory relationship with the community, or more tangible returns such as reduced cost of production, increased sales, raised stock price, or lower headcount requirement. In every case, you must be able to quantify the result in measurable terms for the customer.

4M Qualification: Momentum

What's the compelling reason to buy now?

As sales professionals involved in a complex sale, we tend to focus on when we can get the deal signed. But think about that for a minute. Does the buyer care about when the deal is signed? It's unlikely that he does. More probably, he is interested in when he starts or finishes the implementation. If it is a real opportunity, then there is some compelling factor that is driving the momentum of the buyer's decision process. The factors that drive that compelling event are what you need to uncover:

- Is there a date by which this project has to be completed?
- Does it matter if it slips a few months?
- What's critical about that date?
- What is the compelling reason to buy?
- Does he absolutely have to do this now?
- What's the downside for the company if they don't proceed with the purchase of a product such as yours?
- Will someone lose their job?
- Why will the buyer do it now rather than postpone to a later time?

Maybe regulatory compliance deadlines loom. It could be that the current method of dealing with the issue results in an unprofitable production line or higher cost of sales than is accepted in the industry. There could be a new competitor who has entered the market, requiring a response from your prospect. Perhaps the buying cycle is driven by a financial budget or accounting period. If there is an incumbent supplier, or a product or process that is being replaced, you need to understand, for example, when the maintenance period for that product runs out. The customer will probably want to have their replacement in place by then.

Understanding the buyer's compelling reason to buy, and his committed schedule, helps you to qualify the opportunity. Once you know for sure that you can identify these two, you can be fairly secure that someone will get a deal, and if it's going to be you, you can estimate better when you might get it signed.

Has he got 'skin in the game'?

Good deals are achievable when both the buyer and the seller commit reasonable resources to the buying and selling process. If you are doing all of the work, you need to question whether the 'buyer' is serious about proceeding. Free trials work well with hair shampoo, soda drinks or movie trailers – it is an effective way to reach a mass audience – but it does not work for complex technology sales. Unless the buyer spends time on the evaluation, then you can't get to understand his business problem, the impact on his business of the problem, or the likely benefit that you can deliver. Furthermore, his perception of the value of your time, and that of your colleagues who support you in the sale, is reduced if you continue to give without getting.

Don't work for free. You must always get something in return for your efforts. Ideally, you want to be paid for product trials or an evaluation pilot project. Sometimes that's not possible, but you should at least use a request for a product evaluation as a mechanism to gain further access in the account, or to delve deeper into the buyer's mind:

> "I will get my technical support team to allocate five days to this evaluation. Can we confirm your business objectives again? From your perspective what does success look like? What do we need to prove to get to the next stage? What's the next step, if you are happy with the evaluation? We normally charge for this evaluation, and I would like to do that still, but I'd be willing to offset this charge against a future purchase. Alternatively, can you raise a conditional purchase order that commits an order if we meet the success criteria that you determine for the evaluation?"

Every situation is different and you will need to decide for yourself how far you can guide the customer. You must, however, be sure that you aren't expending resources on the project if the customer isn't also committing effort and time.

What's going to change?

Consider, for example, what happens in the customer's company when it purchases a sales force automation system – behavior change. When a customer purchases any complex or sophisticated product or service, he will only get value with usage, and usage will imply change. Think about the impact in the purchasing department when a new supply chain management solution is implemented – behavior change. What behavior change is necessary if a company adopts the SELECT SELLING methodology?

With SELECT SELLING, the sales force will modify how they interact with customers, having revised how they select their target customers in the first instance. The company as a whole adopts a common language. When a sales person engages his technical support colleagues in a project, he will always be asked whether the prospect is in the company's 'sweet spot'. Sales compensation plans will be modified to motivate the sales person to pursue deals that they know they can win. The whole company will understand the need to get 'layered' in the target customer's organization, with access at multiple levels to all the buying influencers.

If an opportunity is real, the buyer understands the need to change. He may not, as yet, have figured out the transformation that may be necessary, but a smart buyer will wait until he fully comprehends the implications of an implementation, before he signs a deal. It's your job to guide him through that discovery and, through that journey, you demonstrate evidence of your understanding of his business and your ability to create value for him – you become his partner rather than his vendor. If you don't do that, your competitor will, and suddenly you're out of the loop.

FIGURE 29: SELECT SELLING 4MQ MODEL QUALIFICATION QUESTIONS

4MQ Qualification	Qualification Question
Method	Are all the steps in the buying process understood? Are competitive issues understood? Have we engaged with the LOB Manager? Are ALL decision criteria well understood?
Money	Is the budget allocated, authorized and available? Is the budget threatened by competing projects? How was the budget determined? Can we afford to pursue? Can we afford to win?
Motivation	Is the personal motivation for each buying influencer known? Is there a clearly documented description of the business problem that is agreed between you and the buyer? Can we meet the need for each buying influencer? Has an ROI model been agreed with the customer?
Momentum	Is there a compelling reason to buy? Is there a committed implementation date? Has the customer committed resource to the buying project? Is behavior change understood and committed?

CONCLUSION

Borrowing Mike's comment from earlier in the chapter, why work on unqualified opportunities when you could be making money? Using the **SELECT SELLING 4M Qualification Model**, you can weed out losers. Stay focused on Method, Money, Motivation and Momentum to gain a clear and objective perspective on the opportunity. Resources are always limited, and you must choose the deals that you can win. You shouldn't feel good about coming in second place.

CHAPTER SUMMARY: MEMO TO THE SALES SPECIALIST

- Effective qualification, as an integral part of the sales process, is a supremely valuable tool, not just for the sales organization, but for the company overall.
- Poor qualification leads to missed targets, and surprise sales losses; good qualification helps you weed out losers early.
- Qualification is not an event; it's an on-going process. As buyers evaluate you, you must continuously qualify them.
- Use the **SELECT SELLING 4M Qualification Model** to qualify the customer, and to identify information gaps and potential areas of risk in a sale.
- **4MQ – Method:**
  - Understand all the steps in the buying process.
  - Understand competitive issues.
  - Engage with the LOB Manager.
  - Understand ALL decision criteria.
- **4MQ – Money**
  - Is budget allocated, authorized, and available?
  - Check for competing projects.
  - Learn how the budget was determined.
  - Check whether you can win, and whether it's worth winning.
- **4MQ – Motivation**
  - Use the Motivation Matrix to understand the personal motivation for each influencer.
  - Agree, and document, the business problem.
  - Use the Solution Matrix to determine that you can meet the need of each influencer.
  - Agree the ROI model with the customer.
- **4MQ – Momentum**
  - Determine the compelling reason to buy.
  - Assess the resource committed by the customer to the buying process.
  - Understand the behavioral change impact of your solution.

CHAPTER 7

THE SELECT SELLING PIPELINE MANAGEMENT SYSTEM

In the last chapter, we focused on qualification of opportunities, to help you identify which deals you could win. By qualifying opportunities well, you know where to spend your time to meet your quota each month or quarter. But while many companies' financial cycles force measurement in four financial quarters, it's rare that a customer's buying cycle will start and end every three months. Opportunities that you begin work on today may not come to fruition for many quarters. If you're short at the end of a quarter's cycle, and you don't have enough opportunities at the right stage of the buying cycle in your pipeline, you are likely to finish up under quota. Maintaining a strong pipeline, with enough qualified opportunities at each phase in the pipeline, is the only way to avoid the quarter-end crunch that often results in unnecessary discounting, just to make your quarter's number. You should determine how many deals you need to be working on to remove that pressure, close enough sales, and still have something to work with as you build for the next quarter.

PIPELINE STRUCTURE & MANAGEMENT

It is often difficult to decide how many stages you should have in your sales pipeline. We have seen different companies with their pipelines segmented into anything between three and 12 stages (we recommend no more than five) in the pipeline. Every week, or month, sales managers then 'manage' the sales force by working through each individual's sales pipeline to determine how many opportunities are at each stage, and what probability to apply to each opportunity. More often than not, this is a fruitless exercise for two main reasons.

First, subjectivity plays a large part. In most cases, the interpretation of how to categorize the opportunity is left to the salesperson's discretion. The buying cycle is often ignored, and there is usually little linkage between the key qualification questions used, and the stage of the process. One of the benefits of a standardized sales process is that a common language is adopted by everyone in the company involved in the sale. Clear deliverables are linked to each stage of the sale, and overall productivity increases.

Second, it is futile to determine the value of a pipeline by multiplying the value of each opportunity by the probability of it closing. There is no prize for second or third place in selling. You either win the deal or you lose. Having 10 opportunities at 10% probability mathematically may be the equivalent of one full opportunity – but it is not the same as having a signed contract. We are constantly amazed at how seasoned sales managers continue to value their pipelines in this manner. These percentage figures assume a 'steady state' economy, no variance in the competitive landscape, and a constant product scenario. Then the numbers often feed directly into company forecasts. Back to the fairy tale! Having a standardized sales process, and a fully-documented and formally-defined pipeline, with well-understood rules, results in everyone having the same, realistic view of the forecast.

We have designed the **SELECT SELLING** sales process to incorporate stages in the pipeline that reflect the customer's buying cycle. It seems more logical to us to link the selling cycle to the customer's buying cycle, than to use other measures that sometimes seem arbitrary. If you take this approach, the selling actions that you have to plan become self-apparent. You understand the concerns of the buyer at each stage of the buying cycle, and, in effect, your pipeline management becomes a summary sales action plan. In addition, you can now link and layer the qualification process to the overall sales process, to help determine which qualification questions need to be answered, at each stage in the process.

In **Chapter 4**, we segmented the buying cycle into four phases: Requirements, Evidence, Acquisition and Post-Sale. In **SELECT SELLING**, we divide our Pipeline Management System (**Figure 30**) into almost the same four phases, this time replacing 'Post-Sale' with Verbal Order, this being the customer's verbal commitment, or promise, to place the order with you. We also include the initial 'Target Customer Selection' phase at the top of the pipeline. Once you have selected and contacted your target customer, you will proceed to guide him through the Requirements, Evidence, and Acquisition stages of his buying cycle, guiding him to place an order with you. If you sow enough seeds, with enough of these (appropriately targeted) customers, and create value for them, you will optimize your opportunity to reap the benefit.

FIGURE 30: THE SELECT SELLING PIPELINE MANAGEMENT SYSTEM

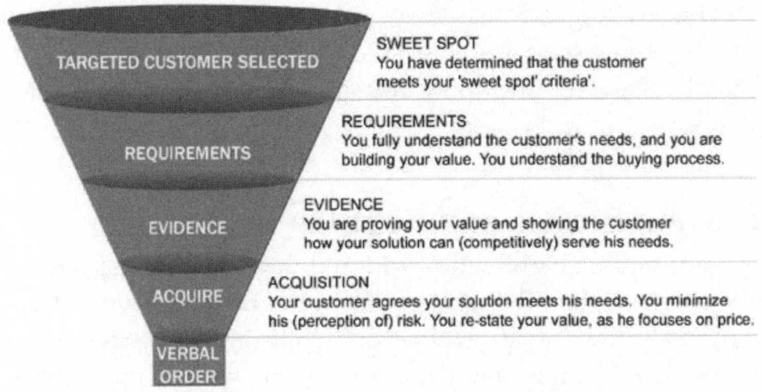

Keep the Funnel Full

You mightn't want to do it, but sometimes you're going to have to generate your own leads. Getting appropriately-targeted customers into the top of your sales funnel is the source of your raw material. Without that raw material, you can't build a pipeline. When there are gaps in your pipeline, pressure builds on the few opportunities you have. You're tempted to try to progress a specific deal too aggressively. Your state of anxiety over this quarter's revenue is heightened by the fact that you are looking into a void for next quarter. It may be the stated role of the marketing department to deliver qualified leads to the salesforce, and you might be one of the fortunate few who is adequately served in this manner, but if you don't recognize the need to look constantly for new opportunities yourself, you lose control over your destiny.

The likelihood of finding a good opportunity is dependent on the type of activity you undertake. If you are a Sales Specialist, you have a broad network of contacts who are potential customers. They respect you and the value you can bring to their business. Your existing customers can provide you with further business within their company, and referrals to their counterparts in similar companies. Strong relationships with industry consultants and analysts are a good source of recommendations for new business opportunities.

Your own market assessment and development activities will always provide the best quality of sales leads, but be sure that the folks in marketing aren't working in a vacuum. Make sure they are in lock-step with your needs. Help them understand what's exciting the customers. Together, you can craft effective seminar programs, and telesales, emarketing, or direct mail, campaigns for your territory. Marketing often bemoans the fact that they generate leads and the salesforce ignores them. Get them on your side by telling them what you need, and then by showing them how you are responding to the good work that they do.

Rocks and Stones and Pebbles

If you want to fill a barrel with rocks and maximize the capacity of the barrel, you have to fill the gaps between the rocks with stones or pebbles. It's the same with your pipeline. Experienced sales professionals will understand that relying on a small number of big deals is risky, and they will balance their opportunity portfolio with smaller deals in order to keep the numbers moving, in case the big rock falls off the cliff. It is one of the truisms of selling: big deals inevitably take longer to close than originally envisioned. Three months becomes six months – or a year. You need to be working on a mix of large deals and smaller opportunities. While waiting for the big deal, no one is making any money and desperation levels increase if there isn't a backup plan. Your negotiation position weakens, and that major opportunity turns into a minor profit deal. Rocks and stones and pebbles make for a full barrel.

THE PIPELINE VALUE FACTOR

There are four factors that determine the health of a sales pipeline:

- Integrity of data
- Deal value
- Number of deals
- Balance across pipeline stages.

The information in the pipeline system must be pristine, continually updated to reflect progress, wins and losses. Everyone must understand the language being used and the salesperson (in particular) must constrain his normal unbridled optimism and not allow himself to overstate the potential value, or proximity to closure, of a deal. Every person entering, or interpreting, data must have a common understanding of the rules being applied to determine where an opportunity sits. Later in this chapter, we suggest how to determine how you might place the opportunities at the appropriate stage of the pipeline.

How long is your typical sales cycle? How much time passes during each phase of the buying cycle? As some customers are working through the Requirements phase of their cycle, you need to have others that you are guiding through the Evidence stage, and more with whom you are finalizing the issues that come up during Acquisition. To keep the pipeline balanced, and maintain a steady deal flow, you need to have an adequate number and value of opportunities at each stage in the pipeline. We use the Pipeline Value Factor, or PVF, to help gauge the value.

To achieve 100% of, say, a quarterly target, consistently over consecutive quarters, PVF is the measure of what multiple of that target number you would need to have in each stage of the pipeline, at any point in time. While PVF doesn't take into consideration the mix of large and small deals, and it is a blunt tool, it is a useful early warning system. If you don't have enough value in your pipeline, then whether it is made up of large or small deals isn't the big problem. The problem is that you don't have enough in your pipeline. PVF is well illustrated by the following story.

Using the Pipeline Value Factor

A client of ours was experiencing what it called 'lumpy sales numbers'. One quarter, it might over-achieve the sales target considerably, while in the next quarter, the salesforce would struggle to make their numbers. Overall, the company was hitting its sales target but, because of the 'lumpiness' of the revenue, it was experiencing cash-flow difficulties in the down quarters. It had to maintain higher levels of support staff, all of the time, in order to deal with the support requirements during the higher revenue quarters. Vince, the Vice President of Sales at the company, asked us to look at their sales process, to see if we could diagnose the cause of the problem and, hopefully, prescribe a solution.

On examination, it appeared that the problem was more prevalent in certain territories than in others and, rather than look at the whole sales organization at once, we decided that we would review a 'problem territory' and compare it with one that was delivering more consistent results. For our purpose here, we will describe what we found with two regional sales managers.

John and Michelle each had a quarterly target of $1 million, and the average sales cycle was about 12 months. Before we reviewed the sales process, we set some time aside, and worked with the upper level sales management, to create a vision of a healthy pipeline for their company. In our experience, most 'lumpy' revenue trends come from weak pipeline management, as weak pipeline management implies poor revenue visibility, and consequently no chance to deal with a projected revenue shortfall.

Working backwards from the overall quarterly revenue target for a territory, we agreed that, at least from a revenue forecast perspective, deals that were in the Requirements or Evidence phases were almost certainly not going to close in the current quarter. Vince also wanted to treat deals in the Acquisition stage as not closing in the quarter. Once a verbal order had been received, it was usual that final contract negotiations would take two months or so. Mike had been burned too many times, by lengthy contractual negotiations, to base his current quarter forecast on deals where the sales person had not yet got the verbal commitment from the customer. That meant that we could only be confident in forecasting opportunities that made it to the Verbal Order stage. At that stage, the sales person, and regional sales manager, were committing to Vince that these deals would happen, having received a verbal commitment from the client.

After much discussion, we resolved to apply a PVF of 150% to the Verbal Order stage. This meant that, even though we had agreed that an opportunity could only get into the Verbal Order box if the customer had verbally committed to placing the order, we felt it appropriate to allow for last minute catastrophes, or delays, in one out of three cases. (Losing one out of three meant we needed a PVF of 150% to have three opportunities in the pipeline to be sure of getting two deals in that quarter.) Until there was a final signed contract, Mike wanted to have some room to maneuver.

We applied a PVF of 300%, 500% and 800% respectively to the Acquisition, Evidence and Requirements stages. It was important to ensure that the pipeline was adequately balanced, as Vince felt that this would drive the company to take a more long-term perspective on business development activity. If that could be achieved, we believed that the quarterly goals could be met consistently, and not only would we take the lumpiness out of the revenue, but we could probably increase the overall revenue - once we provided the necessary education, guidance and assistance to all of the sales team. In addition to tracking the value of the deals in the pipeline, we also wanted to be able to measure the number and mix of opportunities that combined to make up the value.

When we first reviewed the pipeline for John and Michelle (see **Figure 31**), we uncovered fairly clear indicators of what was causing peaks and troughs in the revenue. Michelle's team was working pretty well – she was the 'control group' for this review. It turned out that Michelle had virtually sequestered two members of the marketing group to work on lead generation for her; preparing customers for the Requirements stage of the pipeline – specifically to her specification.

John, on the other hand, had fewer deals going on and, even though the average size of his deal was larger, he was exposed by not having enough balance in his pipeline overall to allow for a loss of any of his large deals. Also, while the average contract value achieved by the company across all deals was $200,000, John had focused his team on opportunities that were likely to result in contracts valued between $500,000 and $1,000,000. The consequence of that, of course, was 'lumpy sales'. If a deal slipped from one quarter to the next, the effect was devastating to John's numbers for the quarter. It also meant that a disproportionate amount of time was being invested in each of those large opportunities, and little attention was being given to filling the funnel.

FIGURE 31: AN EXAMPLE PIPELINE VALUE FACTOR TABLE

Target: $ 1m			John	Michelle
Requirements	PVF: 800%	Number	3	40
		Value	$1.4m	$7.3m
Evidence	PVF: 500%	Number	3	36
		Value	$1.2m	$5.2m
Acquisition	PVF: 300%	Number	8	22
		Value	$4.2m	$3.8m
Verbal Order	PVF: 150%	Number	4	12
		Value	$2.0m	$1.6m

Vince had been using the **SELECT SELLING** pipeline phases. He was categorizing the opportunities by the Requirements, Evidence, Acquisition and Verbal Order phases of the buying/selling cycle, but he had not introduced PVF. Nor was he consciously tracking the number of opportunities making up the potential deal value. By implementing the PVF measure, it highlighted for John and his team the need to 'front-load' his funnel, and achieve a balanced pipeline similar to Michelle's.

By tracking the number of deals, as well as the value, Vince could identify early in the cycle whether John's barrel was full of just rocks, or whether he had the necessary mix of stones and pebbles as well. Through this simple exercise, John felt he could ask for supporting resource to help his business development activities, and he also saw the merit in directing his team to pursue a blend of opportunities.

Creating Your Own Pipeline Management System

If you are using the **Select Selling** methodology, you fill the funnel with prospects that meet your Target Customer Selection, or 'sweet spot', criteria as outlined in **Chapter 3**. Working with those prospects, you need to implement a Pipeline Management System to manage your prospects.

The four **Select Selling** steps to creating your own Pipeline Management System are:

1. Decide on your Qualifiers.
2. Apply Qualifiers to each Pipeline Stage.
3. Calculate your Pipeline Value Factor.
4. Mix the Rocks, Stones and Pebbles.

Decide on your Qualifiers

The **Select Selling** 4M Qualification Model arms you with a set of qualification questions to use as rules, or qualifiers, for your pipeline stages. Extend this list, if you need to. The qualification questions will help you to uncover the customer's needs, to establish how he will evaluate your offering, and to determine who in the account really holds the power.

Apply Qualifiers to each Pipeline Stage

As you know by now, we suggest that you qualify early and qualify hard. Apply as many of the qualifiers to the Requirements and Evidence stages as you feel are necessary to unearth potential showstoppers. If you uncover a problem early, you have a better chance of resolving it. If you can't fix it, it's better to find out early, so that you don't waste time on a deal that you can't win.

Figure 32 shows our recommended qualifiers for Requirements, Evidence, and Acquisition. If you follow our guidelines, you cannot progress a deal from one stage to the next, until you can satisfy all of the requisite qualifiers.

FIGURE 32: PIPELINE STAGE QUALIFIERS

Stage	Qualifiers
Requirements	Are all the steps in the buying process understood? Have we engaged with the LOB Manager? Is there a clearly documented description of the business problem that is agreed between you and the buyer? Is there a committed implementation date? Has the customer committed resource to the buying project?
Evidence	Can we meet the need for each buying influencer? Is the budget allocated, authorized and available? Is the budget threatened by competing projects? Are competitive issues understood? Is there a compelling reason to buy? How was the budget determined? Are ALL decision criteria well understood? Is the personal motivation for each buying influencer known?
Acquisition	Has an ROI model been agreed with the customer? Is behavior change understood and committed? Can we afford to pursue? Can we afford to win?

Calculate your Pipeline Value Factor

Determining what opportunity value you need to factor into each of the pipeline stages is not an exact science, and is best calculated by reference to historical data:

- On average, how long does it take for an opportunity to progress from initial engagement to closure?
- How many of the customers that you had identified this time last year have progressed to further stages of the pipeline?
- How many have closed?
- How many were lost?

As you refine your qualification and selling skills, your close rate will improve and the selling cycle should become shorter. When these changes or any other changes occur, you will need to recalibrate the PVF.

Usually, we find that a certain percentage of deals move quickly, while others seem to take an interminably long time to progress. This is often a consequence of whether a customer has an Unknown, Known or Active need (see **Chapter 5**). The quality of your Target Customer Selection also impacts the rate of progress. If you select customers who are in the center of your 'sweet spot', the sale will be more likely.

In general, we like to see companies adopt a PVF policy that approximates to that used in our example above. This means that you should have a PVF of 800%, 500%, 300%, and 150%, respectively, for the Requirements, Evidence, Acquisition and Verbal Order stages of the pipeline.

Mix the Rocks, Stones and Pebbles

To avoid 'lumpy' sales, you should determine the right mix of rocks, stones and pebbles, by calculating preferred average deal size. Too many opportunities that are larger or smaller than your preferred average deal will likely end in tears.

CONCLUSION

Developing a sales forecast generally isn't much fun, but getting it wrong means that you are spending time doing something you don't like – and you're still not getting any benefit. An effective pipeline management system, consistently executed, provides clarity and visibility which, together, give you greater control over your destiny. A true pipeline provides an early warning system; it shows where you are strong and points to areas that need attention. Use our system or develop your own. Use it well and it will bring you an uncommon freedom to focus on what you have to do today in order to achieve your revenue targets consistently, without the interminable stress that accompanies uncertainty.

With the **SELECT SELLING Pipeline Management System**, we try to remove subjectivity from the process. Wherever the opportunity is in the pipeline, that should be where it belongs, without reference to personal opinion or perspective. Each salesperson, sales manager or sales executive should understand a common language, and therefore, by extension, each should have the same view of the health of the pipeline. If fully adopted and rigorously applied, an effective pipeline management system all but removes the need for those fruitless weekly, or monthly, review cycles. Sales meetings should therefore become more about problem-solving, brainstorming, and resolving issues or addressing obstacles, than about reporting sales progress. Sales meetings become sales action planning meetings, rather than painful information review exercises. A common sales report, generated either by a sales force automation program configured to use this system or by an agreed manual reporting approach, should provide sufficient progress information. Line-by-line opportunity review by sales managers, trying to eke out or uncover information, should become obsolete, as everyone seeks to add value to the sale rather than spend time trying to figure out what's going on.

In the next chapter, we link in the sales actions that you might need to take as you progress an opportunity through the funnel. There is a strong relationship between the qualification process described in **Chapter 6** and the stages of progress set out here. You will need to decide for yourself whether this works for you, but please be dispassionate about creating qualification rules. Set the bar high enough to disqualify mediocre opportunities.

CHAPTER SUMMARY:
MEMO TO THE SALES SPECIALIST

- Maintaining a strong pipeline, with enough qualified opportunities at each phase in the pipeline, is the only way to avoid the quarter-end crunch.
- One of the benefits of a standardized sales process is that a common language is adopted by everyone in the company. Clear deliverables are linked to each stage of the sale, and overall productivity increases.
- We recommend no more than five stages in the pipeline.
- It is futile to determine the value of a pipeline by multiplying the value of each opportunity by the probability of it closing.
- You must generate your own leads. If you don't look constantly for new opportunities, you lose control over your destiny.

- If you want to fill a barrel with rocks and maximize the usage of the capacity of the barrel, you have to fill the gaps between the rocks with stones or pebbles. It's the same with your pipeline.
- The **SELECT SELLING Pipeline Management System** has five stages: Target Customer Selection, Requirements, Evidence, Acquisition and Verbal Order.
- Qualifiers are used to determine where in the pipeline you should place an opportunity.
- You need to have enough opportunities at each stage of the pipeline. Use the **Pipeline Value Factor** (PVF) to help you calculate the value you need.
- To create your own pipeline management system, decide on your qualifiers, apply qualifiers to each pipeline stage, calculate your PVF and get the right mix of rocks, stones and pebbles.
- An effective pipeline management system, consistently executed, provides clarity and visibility, which together give you greater control over your destiny.

CHAPTER 8

IMPLEMENTING SELECT SELLING: SALES ACTION PLANNING

SELLING IS A JOURNEY

Selling a complex solution to a large corporation is a multi-layered, multi-event journey. It's a science not an art, and science is a discipline. At every step, you need to assess your position, determine the next optimum destination, and develop a map to get you there, calling on supporting resources as necessary. As you reach critical milestones, you must re-evaluate, re-calibrate and adjust your plans to adapt to the changing environment. It was Abraham Lincoln who said:

> "If I had nine hours to chop a tree, I'd spend the first six sharpening my axe."

Planning each step of the sale gives you the opportunity to take control of the sales process, without overtly taking control of the buyer. At each juncture, you need to view things from the customer's perspective:

- What is to the forefront of his mind right now?
- Is it risk, features, value, timing, price, or a combination of all of these?

Understanding what the customer wants to achieve, and delivering to those requirements, opens the door for you to make progress towards you own goals.

You must have a plan. If you don't, it's hard to know whether you are making any progress or not. You don't know whether you are winning or losing. If you don't have a map of the journey you want the customer to take, you will be forced to use *his* guidelines, and you will lose control. In **Chapter 4**, we discussed the typical corporate buying process. What are your strategies and tactics that accommodate the buyer's process, but guide him towards your own milestones?

Remember too the changing perspective of the buyer, as he moves from the Requirements phase of the buying process through Evidence, Acquisition and Post-Sale (see **Figure 17, Chapter 4**). Depending on the current phase of the cycle, your sales actions and qualification questions change (see **Figure 18, Chapter 4**). The more time you can afford to spend on preparation for your next meeting, the better chance you have of taking the right action. And don't be sure you have all of the answers yourself. Bounce alternative tactics off your colleagues or management and play out different scenarios.

Every Opportunity has a Critical Risk

Think about the most important opportunity that you are working on today. If you just now received a call, or more likely an email, to inform you that you lost the sale, can you list the three most likely reasons why that happened?

In most cases, salespeople lose deals, not because of product price or features, but because they have been outsold. One of your competitors has done a better job of convincing the customer that his solution is a better fit for the customer's requirements, or the customer has declined to proceed with the project, because he has not been convinced of the return on investment, or he has decided not to give you the order, because he is not comfortable with you, your product or your company. We call this the **Critical Risk**. If you were to lose the sale today, what would be the most likely reason?

Give the Critical Risk some thought every time you consider the opportunity and, if you assess your position honestly, you will uncover risks in time to do something about them. If, from the customer's perspective (and that's the only one that counts), you have a gap in your solution, maybe you can find a partner to fill the gap. If the customer isn't convinced about your value, perhaps you can leverage a successful reference customer to convince this prospect, or develop strong ROI analysis. If there appear to be concerns about your company, a visit from a member of the executive team, sometimes, can help to assuage the customer's concerns. Often, the customer just wants to know that they have a senior person in your company who is 'on their side'.

EVERY SALE NEEDS A PLAN

Developing a Sales Action Plan is a way to define the tactics that you need to deliver your strategy for each customer acquisition, or each sale closure. It is designed to provoke honest thought, as you assess the prospective sales situation. It provides the momentum to help you decide what you want to achieve, and to visualize the journey you want to take.

One of the problems we frequently see in sales plans is that they start with a target date for closing the sale and work backwards from there. While it is important to have a timed and measurable sales objective, the difficulty with starting with the close date is that there is an incredible tendency to skip all of the stages up to that. Also, the buyer is rarely focused on the date by which he has to sign the Purchase Order. His concern is his implementation date, or his 'go-live' schedule. When you start with the close date, you are immediately out of sync with the buyer. Then your forecast is off track, and suddenly you're under pressure to close the deal too early. As soon as you do that, your relationship with the customer deteriorates and you've taken the first step on the slippery slope to losing the deal.

When asked about his incredible shot-making ability, Jack Nicklaus, possibly the greatest golfer of all time, described his thought process:

> "I start by assessing where I am, looking at the lie of the ball, figuring out the terrain, gauging how far I am from the hole, and thinking about the wind and other elements of the weather. Then I decide where I want the ball to land so that it ends up near the hole or at the right place on the fairway. Next I visualize the flight-path of the ball and see in my mind the kind of swing I'm going to have to make to get the ball to travel on that flight-path. Then I make that swing."

Just like Jack, you need to visualize each bounce of the ball before you make your next swing. You need to assess the terrain. Figure out where you're starting from. Decide what you want to achieve, where you want the ball to land, always being sure that you avoid the traps or hazards. Like golf, a lot of what effective selling is about happens before you take your first action. Before you put your mouth or pen in gear, you need to exercise your mind. The other thing about Jack – he practiced a lot.

The SELECT SELLING Sales Action Plan

The **SELECT SELLING** Sales Action Plan Worksheet is one of the most used of the **SELECT SELLING** Sales tools, and we will use it as a framework for this chapter.

As you can see from **Figure 33**, your Sales Action Plan identifies the account, the owner of the account (that's you), the pipeline stage and the date. Additionally, it sets out the objectives of the plan, the tactics or actions required, and the resources that are needed to execute those tactics.

FIGURE 33: AN EXAMPLE SALES ACTION PLAN

Account Name: ABC International
Owner: John Smith
Pipeline Stage: Requirements
Date: Sep 14

Objective & Tactics	Resources	Date	Status
Confirm Buyer Perspective			
1. Document business problem & get agreement from LOB Mgr	JS	Sep 17	Done
2. Interview CFO & Evaluator	JS, Sales Eng.	Sep 24	
3. Propose engagement framework	JS	Sep 24	
Demonstrate Solution Value			
1. Create ROI Paper	Mkt, Fin	Sep 22	
2. Present case study	JS, Mkt	Sep 24	
3. Competitive Analysis	JS, Mkt	Sep 28	
4. Provide customized usage scenario document for client	JS	Sep 27	
5. Schedule technical evaluation	JS, Sales Eng	Sep 24	

You should always write down the plan. We find that a simple template format (incorporated into your sales force automation program, or used in a Word or Excel document) is quick to use and eases the process. (A softcopy of the SELECT SELLING Sales Action Plan template is available on www.selectselling.com.) It gives you opportunities to share the action plan with colleagues on whom you depend, and forces you to build a realistic timeline. If you are managing a number of accounts simultaneously, you've got to keep track of a lot of information. Having to document the details helps clarify your thinking, and lessens the chance of missing something.

Before you can decide on your objectives or tactics, you need to assess the status, or health, of the current opportunity. A detailed, and honest, situation analysis can help you achieve that.

SITUATION ANALYSIS

Developing your Sales Action Plan is an iterative process. As the context evolves, and the opportunity progresses through the different stages of the buying/selling cycle, the result of your Situation Analysis will vary, and your consequent objectives and tactics will change, as shown in **Figure 34**.

FIGURE 34: SITUATION ANALYSIS

	SELECT SELLING Qualification Actions	Objectives, Tactics, Resources	SELECT SELLING Actions	SELECT SELLING Tools
Requirements	• Are all the steps in the buying process understood? • Have we engaged with the LOB Manager? • Is there a clearly documented description of the business problem that is agreed between you and the buyer? • Is there a committed implementation date? • Has the customer committed resource to the buying project?	Use the outcome of the Situation Analysis, and the guidance of the Selling Actions, to determine your own 'account specific' Objectives, Tactics and Resource requirements.	• Educate the customer on the benefit of change. • Understand the customer's pain and business impact of that pain. • Test their understanding of the benefits of change and their desire to invest in a solution. • Create value in the mind of the customer by articulating business benefit. • Focus the customer on the important aspects you want considered for evaluation. • Agree a buying cycle framework with checkpoints and mutual resource investment.	• Progressive Questioning Control Model • 4M Qualification Model • Pipeline Management Model

	SELECT SELLING Qualification Actions	Objectives, Tactics, Resources	SELECT SELLING Actions	SELECT SELLING Tools
Evidence	• Can we meet the need for each buying influencer? • Is the budget allocated, authorized and available? • Is the budget threatened by competing projects? • Are competitive issues understood? • Is there a compelling reason to buy? • How was the budget determined? • Are ALL decision criteria well understood? • Is the personal motivation for each buying influencer known?	Use the outcome of the Situation Analysis, and the guidance of the Selling Actions, to determine your own 'account specific' Objectives, Tactics and Resource requirements.	• Show value through demonstrations and description of other successful customers in their industry. • Show value through your understanding of the application of your offering to their business, contextualized for their particular company. • Highlight competitive advantage to be gained over their competition and demonstrate your competitive value over your competition. • Articulate benefits to be delivered by you, your company and your product and test their understanding of these benefits. • Work with the customer to understand the Return on Investment to be gained. • Establish any perceived risk to budget, project momentum or from competitive threats. • Understand their perspective on your position relative to your competitor and the value they perceive the competitor brings. • Confirm progress against the agreed buying cycle framework.	• Progressive Questioning Control Model • Power Gauge • Sales Planning Worksheet • 4M Qualification Model • Pipeline Management Model

	Select Selling Qualification Actions	Objectives, Tactics, Resources	Select Selling Actions	Select Selling Tools
Acquisition	• Has an ROI model been agreed with the customer? • Is behavior change understood & committed? • Can we afford to pursue? Can we afford to win?	Use the outcome of the Situation Analysis, and the guidance of the Selling Actions, to determine your own 'account specific' Objectives, Tactics and Resource requirements.	• Understand the risks the customer perceives and articulate a risk plan to lessen those risks. • Restate your value. • Facilitate reference calls or visits with other customers. • Restate your commitment to partnership with the customer. • Restate competitive position. • Confirm progress against the agreed buying cycle framework.	• Negotiation Model • Power Gauge • Sales Planning Worksheet • 4M Qualification Model • Pipeline Management Model
Verbal Offer	• Has a verbal order been received?	Use the outcome of the Situation Analysis, and the guidance of the Selling Actions, to determine your own 'account specific' Objectives, Tactics and Resource requirements.	• Follow up with the customer to make certain his needs are being met and progress is as per expectation. • Co-ordinate resources within your organization to resolve issues quickly. • Maintain frequent communication with the customer to show your continued interest in his success. • Continue to develop your relationship with the customer for future mutual gain. • After the close, when all is going well, ask for a referral.	

IMPLEMENTING THE SALES ACTION PLAN

Once you have a clear picture of the current landscape, determined by your Situation Analysis, you can define the next set of sales objectives. These objectives should be SMART: Specific; Measurable; Achievable; Realistic; and Timed.

Objectives are what you want to achieve. Placed in the context of the overall sales plan, you can now set time-bounded deadlines for each action to be taken. Each sales objective must have associated tactics or actions that need to be taken to achieve the objective. You should ask yourself what issues, internal to the customer, impact on what you are trying to achieve, and how you might address those issues. You must determine what resources you will need from your own company, to help you achieve the objective. Each tactic should have a scheduled date, and an owner – the person within your company that is responsible for that action. As you make steps forward in the sale, the context of your analysis will change, and the cycle starts all over again.

FIGURE 35: THE STAGES IN SALES ACTION PLANNING

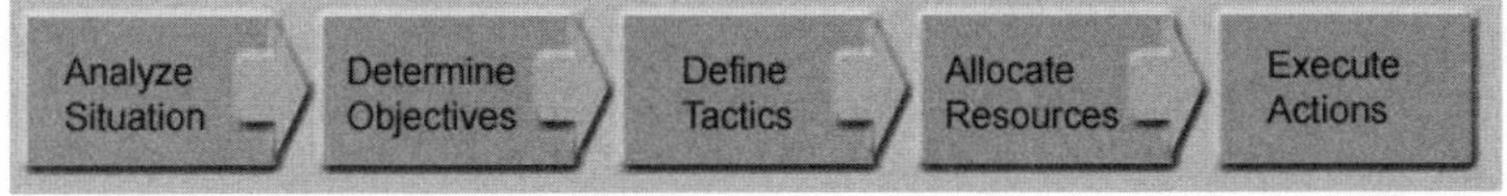

Requirements Stage

If you are not working on a good opportunity – one that you can win – this is when you want to find out. Here, you will determine how well the customer understands his requirements, whether his need is Unknown, Known or Active, how deeply the problem impacts the customer's organization, what the buying process is, and whether the customer truly has a vision of the benefits a solution such as yours might deliver. This stage is the best opportunity you have to shape the need, develop the requirements, and guide the customer along your chosen path, assuming that you can show potential business benefit to be gained from purchasing your solution.

You must question well and listen deeply. Before you can move an opportunity from the prospect stage – a customer who meets your target customer selection criteria – to a qualified prospect that deserves a place in the Requirements stage of your pipeline, you must have engaged with the main LOB Manager to understand the level of need and pain. And, it's not enough just to have spoken with him. You need to have an agreed and documented description of the problem he is trying to solve. You must be sure that he is truly engaged in a buying process, having committed resources to that process, with a targeted implementation date. Understanding his buying cycle and process, you should agree a buying/selling framework that demonstrates mutual resource investment. You should feel good about your ability to meet his needs.

You will recall that, in **Chapter 4**, we highlighted the selling actions that you must engage in at each stage of the buying cycle. We revisit them here and couple them with the corresponding qualification questions for each stage of the pipeline. The actions are used to help develop the Sales Action Plan.

Evidence Stage

As the customer is now engaged in the evidence collection process, gathering data and evidence that your solution can satisfy his requirements, you should be qualifying his ability to buy. You're investing a little further in rounding out his requirements and testing whether he can visualize how your solution is his best choice. To achieve that, your time is spent in creating and demonstrating value, working jointly with the customer to arrive at the best solution. Competitive issues will undoubtedly arise. Your activity should be focused on highlighting your competitive advantage through the creative application of your product or service. You must demonstrate that you can meet the buyer's needs better than your competitor. You will begin work on establishing his return on investment from purchasing your product, though that may well only be finalized in the Acquisition stage.

At this stage, you should understand the hierarchy of influence in the customer's organization, and have agreed with each influencer his motivation and 'hot buttons'. You must be clear about how you can meet the needs of each of these influencers. Experienced buyers will not want you to know whether you are winning or losing. If you know you are winning, you will be more inclined to be firm on your price. If you're losing, and you know it, you will drop out, and the buyer loses leverage against your competition. You must, however, use the relationship you have developed with the internal champion to determine your competitive position. If you don't know how you are faring competitively, you are always at risk.

Now that you have invested considerable time working with the customer, you are entitled to know all of the decision criteria that will be applied to the evaluation. You should ask whether the buyer has an evaluation scorecard that they are using, and underline the resource commitment that you are making if the buyer is unwilling to share it. Use some of the techniques outlined in the Progressive Questioning Control Model, to determine whether the project is at risk, from budget cuts, or competing projects.

Most importantly, you must understand the 'compelling reason to buy'.

Acquisition Stage

Now is the time to stay particularly close to the customer. From his perspective, this is the time of highest risk and you must act accordingly. Thus far, the customer has been engaged with you, outlining his needs and, determining whether your solution can meet those needs. You should revisit your CVP statement, and once again ensure that the customer is satisfied that you are the best choice. Price negotiations will begin, and you should be clear that he understands his costs, and your entire value. Before he will give you the order, he is likely to review the return on investment, or ROI, that will accrue. If applicable, ROI must be calculated for each of the influencers. You may need to return to some of the 'proof points' already established, making sure of your competitive position, testing once more that the value you bring is well understood, and that it meets the requirements of the customer.

We mentioned before that, when a buyer adopts a complex solution, there will be some change in how his company operates. As you uncovered and developed the buyer need, you should have established what behavior change is required. Before the buyer places his order, he will almost certainly have developed his own vision of the requisite changes. You must re-assess his commitment to change, for this is often where deals get delayed, postponed or cancelled. Commitment to change is particularly relevant, if any of your return is dependent on his successful adoption or transaction level. For example, this is sometimes the case when you are delivering your solution on a 'usage or transaction-based' pricing model.

Verbal Order Stage

There is only one test here. Has the buyer given you a verbal order? Are you fully confident that you will get the deal and that you can deliver a signed contract this quarter? Have you checked each of the influencers?

You should review any 'revenue recognition' issues, or policies, that your company has in place, to be sure that you are committing to a revenue number that the company can count. For example, if your deal includes an annual maintenance contract, in addition to a software license purchase, how will the maintenance contract be treated? Are you concerned with total contract value (sometimes termed bookings value), or should you be measuring the recognizable revenue number?

The only reason you should lose the sale at this point is if there are some unreasonable contract terms required by the customer. By understanding the complete buying process from the outset, you should have been able to identify this issue earlier and hopefully address or deflect it.

For each stage in the pipeline, we recommend qualification questions, to use as part of your Situation Analysis. We then suggest selling actions that may be necessary to meet your objectives, and we note the SELECT SELLING tools that you should use (see **Figure 35**).

CONCLUSION

It's all about execution! Lest we lead you astray, we must caution against mistaking a strategic plan for an execution solution. While the plan might well determine the strategy, it's the execution tactics, or actions, that deliver the solution. A good game plan, without high-quality execution, is worthless.

We raise this point having seen companies develop a generic strategic sales plan, then ask their salesforce to modify it for the salesperson's individual account. In that scenario, execution issues often don't get the necessary attention. We prefer to see the salesforce involved in creating a centrally-developed plan, if there is to be a 'standard' one. Not only does the salesperson gain from the exercise, but the company gets to leverage the experience of the seasoned sales professionals. After all, they are the people who have most direct contact with the customers. Also, the individual sales executive is then in a better position to adapt the plan to the situation at hand, having completed the Situation Analysis himself.

CHAPTER SUMMARY: MEMO TO THE SALES SPECIALIST

- Selling is a journey. At every step, you need to re-assess your position.
- You **must** have a plan. If you don't, it's hard to know whether you are making any progress. You don't know if you are winning or losing.
- Every opportunity has a critical risk. Figure out what it is, and what to do about it.
- Sales plans should **not** start with a target planned close date.
- You should always write your plan down.
- Before you can decide on the objectives or tactics of the plan, you need to conduct a rigorous **Situation Analysis**.
- Developing your **Sales Action Plan** is an iterative process with five steps: Analyze Situation; Determine Objectives; Define Tactics; Allocate Resources; and Execute Actions.
- **Objectives** should be SMART: Specific; Measurable; Achievable; Realistic; and Timed.
- Each **Tactic** should have a scheduled date, and an owner – the person within your company who is responsible for that action.
- **SELECT SELLING** recommends qualification questions as part of the Situation Analysis, as well as selling actions and sales tools, as part of the execution, for each of the stages of the pipeline: Requirements; Evidence; Acquisition; and Verbal Order. Use these recommendations or extend them with your own.
- While the plan might well determine the strategy, it's the execution tactics, or actions, that deliver the solution. A good game plan, without high-quality execution, is worthless.

CHAPTER 9

THE CONTINUOUS ART OF COMPLETE NEGOTIATION

Good negotiators are effective persuaders, deep listeners and proficient tacticians. **Complete Negotiators** are also strategists. They have perfected the art of crafting value-creating agreements that reflect the other party's true interests, rather than his bargaining position. Complete Negotiators are concerned with substance more than style. They are cognizant of the plays that occur away from the negotiating table, and have mastered the art of controlling the ground-rules to create a more favorable environment.

Like all components of the **SELECT SELLING** methodology, the negotiation strategies and tactics we recommend involve due preparation. Complete Negotiators recognize that the attitudes of a customer at the negotiation table are often a result of the selling actions taken throughout the sales cycle. If you're subservient or passive in your early engagement with a prospective customer, it is likely that the customer will control the negotiation, as you try to finalize a deal. Negotiation starts early and, in truth, never finishes. Your interaction with the prospective customer colors his negotiating style, and your final bargaining, prior to conclusion of a contract, is just the end of the beginning of your relationship.

Traditional sales techniques teach negotiation as a component of closing the sale. **SELECT SELLING** espouses a more continuous approach. At every step in the selling cycle, Sales Specialists are negotiating. They may be bartering information, negotiating access to other influencers in an account, or trading a 'free trial product' for a competitive assessment from the customer. But they are always negotiating.

Your objective in any negotiation should be to find a positive middle ground – a position where you are happy with the resolution, and your customer is satisfied enough to do the deal. This chapter explores the basic dynamics of negotiation, describes key principles to observe, and sets out some techniques to help you become a Complete Negotiator. It will help you negotiate more confidently, reach agreement with less resistance and conflict, and get better deals.

THE NEGOTIATION ZONE

Negotiation is an interactive and iterative process. It occurs when someone wants something from someone else. In a business or sales context, the vendor has a product or service that the buyer wants. The buyer has money that the vendor wants. Put simply, the buyer negotiates for the maximum product for the minimum price. Conversely, the vendor wants to receive the maximum payment for the minimum deliverable. In the middle of these two extremes is the **Negotiation Zone** (**Figure 36**), where the two parties bargain.

FIGURE 36: THE NEGOTIATION ZONE

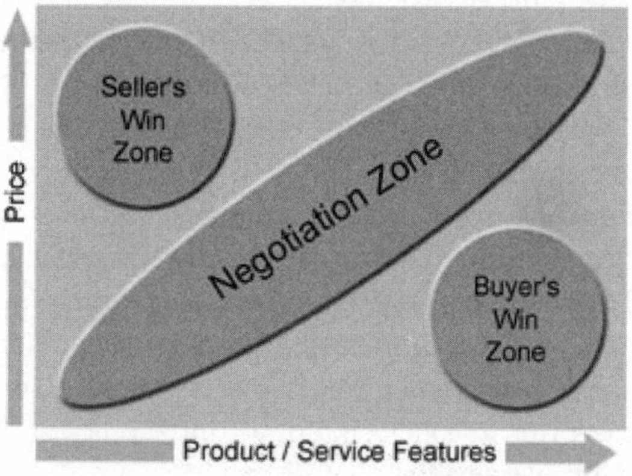

In both simple and complex negotiations, people tend to end up at the mid-point between the two parties' starting positions, assuming equally competent negotiators. It is important, therefore, that you expend disproportionate time evaluating where in the Negotiation Zone you choose to begin. If you're 'too reasonable', you may end up getting less than you might. If you adopt an extreme position, you run the risk of upsetting your opponent and setting the negotiation off on a combative track, and you don't want to do that. Assuming you view negotiation as the start of a longer term relationship, a co-operative negotiation is much healthier.

As you play in the Negotiation Zone, you want your starting point to be your maximum plausible position. Research on setting negotiation goals discloses a simple but powerful fact. The more clarity you have of your negotiation goal, and the more committed you are to achieving that goal, the more likely you are to achieve it. Spend time developing higher expectations for yourself. You can do significantly better without putting the relationship at risk. Your starting position should be greater than you hope to achieve, and the maximum that you feel is plausible. Assuming you have followed SELECT SELLING principles, you will have clearly articulated and demonstrated your value. Any negotiating tactic must build on that value, showing a rationale for your position, rather than appearing arbitrary. It's sometimes a battle of cogency. If you are logical and rational as you demonstrate value, you are more likely to achieve your goal, than if your demands seem disconnected to the value you deliver.

Negotiation is information exchange, explicit bargaining, and commitment. The Negotiation Zone is where you get what you negotiate, not what you deserve. The single most important rule in negotiation is to determine your starting point. Without a clearly-considered, well-supported, and rationalized opening position, you will be forced to back into uncomfortable, 'credibility-losing' and ultimately unprofitable justifications.

THE VALUE TUSSLE

It is clear that the Professional Buyer's job is to get the best possible deal for his company. Note that we said 'get the best possible deal', not 'get the lowest price'. Smart buyers will seek to lower your price, but they will also recognize (with your help) that final contract negotiation should be the start, not the end, of a relationship. It was John Ruskin, one of the great Victorian thinkers, who said:

> "It is unwise to pay too much, but it is also unwise to pay too little. When you pay too much you lose a little money; that is all. When you pay too little; you sometimes lose everything, because the thing you bought was incapable of doing the thing you bought it to do."

Smart Buyers don't necessarily want to squeeze every little last drop of blood out of the deal. They understand the value of reciprocity and that fairness begets fairness. They know that you will be more inclined to support them after the sale, if the deal is a true win-win – though they will never want you to know that.

Other buyers, the **Value Extractors**, see their role purely in terms of 'value denial' and price minimization. They engage continuously in the **Value Tussle** (**Figure** 37), using every opportunity to make you lower your price, or improve your offering. If you offer them a 10% discount, they will look for 20%. If you agree to their 20% discount request, they will want extended payment terms. When you agree to their payment terms, they will look for dedicated support staff, or a future price guarantee. As long as you keep giving, the Value Extractors will keep taking.

FIGURE 37: THE VALUE TUSSLE

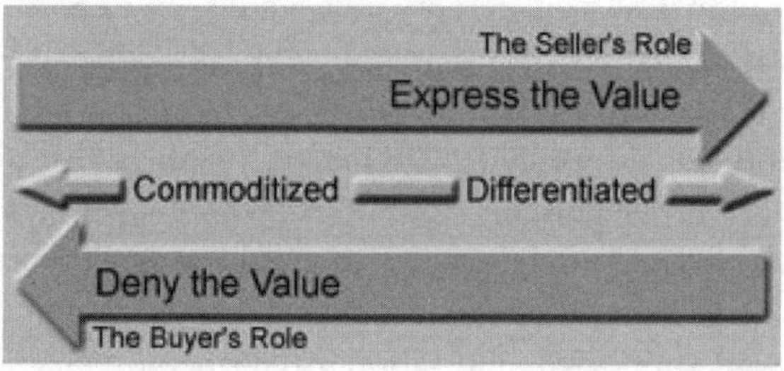

The Seller's Role
Express the Value
Commoditized
Differentiated
Deny the Value
The Buyer's Role

When dealing with Value Extractors, you have to know when, and how, to say "No". Saying "No" can be difficult if you are depending on the deal to make quota or meet a commission threshold. But if you agree to unreasonable demands from a Value Extractor, you are unlikely to ever make money in that account. It is important when dealing with such a buyer that you *want*, not *need*, the deal – and the surest way to find yourself in that position is if you have other deals you can pursue. This underlines the importance of a full pipeline, as outlined in **Chapter** 7.

If you have not engaged with the procurement or legal professionals in your customer's company, and they become involved in the negotiation, they will undoubtedly assume the role of Value Extractor. In that instance, you should never negotiate alone. Your buyer, or sponsor, needs to be at your side of the table, explaining the value that you have convinced him you will deliver. He (the buyer) will want to do that, as he will be focused on maintaining his relationship with your company.

Whether you are dealing with a Smart Buyer or a Value Extractor, you must expect to engage in a Value Tussle. Approaching either of these negotiators, you must understand that your attitude to the negotiation is critical. You should believe that everything is negotiable. Your level of preparedness will greatly impact the outcome. You must embrace the buyer's perspective and adopt a real and demonstrated willingness to listen. Finally, you must maintain a commitment to personal integrity, to reinforce your sense of fairness. It gives you the strength to walk away when you should.

THE COMPLETE NEGOTIATOR

The most commonly-recognized barriers to a negotiated agreement are:

- Poor communication
- Diverse or uncovered interests
- Combative bargaining styles.

Apart from these well-understood obstacles, there exists a more powerful force in negotiation that, all too often, receives little attention: negotiation setup. Inexperienced negotiators, ignorant of the correct framework, will often negotiate the wrong issues, at the wrong time, or in the wrong sequence, frustrating the buyer and damaging their own credibility. They will sometimes negotiate with the wrong representative of the buyer's organization, trying to close someone who doesn't have the authority to do the deal. Concessions given at this juncture are inherited by the 'real buyer' without achieving anything in return.

Complete Negotiators are entrepreneurs, creatively assessing the landscape, to understand how to shape the structure of the negotiation. Much of their negotiation is done away from the negotiation table. They ensure that they deal with the right people and negotiate the right issues, by having controlled the expectations and parameters of the negotiation, before sitting down to bargain. Taking this proactive approach, Complete Negotiators change the playing field to suit their game-plan. They focus not just on the tactics or value in the deal, but plan and strategize, to control and contain the scope and sequence of the negotiations. They prepare their game-plan well in advance, developing their alternative options, while they discover the true interests of their opponent. Prior to the formal negotiation, they seek to uncover any elements of the proposed deal that are likely to prove troublesome, and they consider potential approaches to resolve or deflect those potential conflicts.

In the world of complex sales and SELECT SELLING, Complete Negotiators are Sales Specialists. They are value creators for their customer. They proclaim that value when faced with their negotiator, shifting discussion from price to value. Combining deal setup skills with the traditional negotiation practices of tactics and deal design, Complete Negotiators think laterally, seeking out possible components of a deal that meet the interests of the buyer, but don't impact on their own goal. Uncovering the buyer's true interests, the Complete Negotiator works backwards from there, creating solutions to meet those interests. They're focused, not on the perception of who wins, but on achieving their own goals. It's the 'fame and fortune' thing. Complete Negotiators are focused on the fortune.

THE PRINCIPLES OF NEGOTIATION

Be True to Yourself

It surprises us sometimes to see some sales professionals, who are normally pleasant and reasonable, become aggressive, unruly or perceptibly arrogant when they sit at the negotiation table. In truth they are usually just nervous. Having been schooled in harsh closing techniques, or outmoded negotiation maneuvers, they lose a lot of the ground they had gained when they built a relationship with the customer through the selling cycle.

Inevitably, there will be some confrontation in any negotiation and some sales professionals just don't feel comfortable dealing with it. They adopt a negotiation persona as a defense mechanism. But neither they, nor the customer, are comfortable with this new personality. We counsel you to be yourself – but be the best self you can be. You're the person the customer has asked to be at the table. If you're not comfortable negotiating, you're going to want to get it over with fast, and are likely to give too many concessions too easily, or be overly aggressive in trying to close the deal. More likely, however, once you come to accept that all negotiation styles don't involve screaming or slamming your fist on the desk, you can come to adopt a negotiating style that reflects your personality. Most successful negotiation comes from co-operative communication, not combative posturing. You can still take strong positions and disagree politely. Offering alternatives, while respecting your customer's perspective, but showing reasons why you see things differently, is not being difficult or aggressive. It reflects a confidence in your offering and belief in the value you deliver.

If you feel you need help in a particular negotiation, ask for it. If you are a reticent negotiator, and you are on your own, we advise you to pretend that you are negotiating for someone else. Whatever you concede, you will have to explain and if you don't negotiate what you should, getting true value for your product, you must justify the result to that 'someone'. If you do this, you'll prepare adequately, know what's reasonable to expect – and you won't settle for less.

Embrace the Buyer's Perspective

You must understand and respect the buyer's perspective. Respect his role in the negotiation. By showing him that you are reliable and trustworthy, by not adopting manipulative or underhand tactics, usually you will find a reciprocity that rewards fairness with fairness. You're also then entitled to let him know if you think you are being treated unreasonably. Unfair treatment, left untrammeled, breeds exploitation and the ultimate collapse of the relationship – whether you get the deal or not.

Negotiations often break down because one party has a 'bottom-line' position that the other doesn't believe is 'fair'. But 'fair' is a range, and the scope of fairness is quite dependent on perspective. If you meet your customer 'half-way' in a negotiation, then you need to be sure that he sees it as half-way. The bias inherent in the buyer's (or seller's) role can sometimes distort the vision of fairness. Negotiation is a very personal experience, even for experienced negotiators. Reaching agreement is rarely an easily-visualized journey. If the final position were easy to see, it would make negotiation redundant. As you prepare to adopt your maximum plausible starting point, you must allow for the buyer's perception of your position, recognizing that partisan perspectives quickly become irreconcilable.

The buyer's role changes in the negotiation process. As he enters the Acquisition phase of the buying cycle, risk is to the forefront of his mind. Some things are easier for him to concede than others, and you should probe to understand his real wants. Reverse sides and look at things from his side of the table. How will he justify the deal to his boss? If he has a problem, then it's your problem too. Share the problem and help him solve it. Find a middle ground that satisfies both your requirement and his, by understanding his true interests. To do that, you must understand how he sees his basic negotiation problem. To change the other side's mind, you need to get inside it. Put yourself in his shoes. Showing him the path to agreement, rather than pushing him towards your destination, is generally more productive.

Traditional negotiators sometimes adopt a 'devil-may-care' attitude, disregarding the other party's concerns, interests and fears. Not only does this breed bad-will, but it undermines your ability to understand their problem and influence the resolution. As a Sales Specialist, you've expended a lot of energy in creating value for your customer. Now is not the time to abandon that approach. Don't assume an unco-operative persona prepared to do battle, rather than to resolve conflict. Be the guy working with the customer to find a solution, rather than the guy with a polarized view, driving the deal from the other side of the table.

If you're having difficulty reaching agreement on a particular negotiation point, be proactive in finding an answer, by asking the buyer how he visualizes a solution. You probably will not like what you hear, but you will learn about his position, and he will feel good about your open approach. Mutual participation in the process engenders a sense of trust. It's not enough to know what you want from the negotiation. You need to understand what your customer wants. To be a Complete Negotiator, you should also try to figure out what he thinks you want.

Look Beyond Price

We stated earlier in this book that, unless value is established in the mind of the buyer, any price is too high. Before you begin to negotiate price, you need to be sure that price is the only issue left to discuss. Traditional sales executives will often use price as their main closing tool. Usually it's ineffective – or, at best, results in marginally profitable business. If the buyer asks to negotiate price, and you have been in a competitive selling situation, confirm that you are the preferred supplier in advance of the price negotiations. Unless you receive that confirmation, you should ask that discussions on price be deferred until the buyer is convinced that you have the best solution. Price is easiest for the buyer to negotiate. For you, the sales person, you can only bring your price down – never up. If you discuss price earlier in the process than you should, then any price concessions you give become the starting point for the next round of negotiation – if you actually become the selected supplier.

> Gerry works for a large software company and has responsibility for selling his company's products to banks all over the world. When competitive situations arise, he is usually the larger player, battling it out with smaller, sometimes more nimble, and usually cheaper, competitors. When price objections arise, as they invariably do, Gerry points out the financial stability of his own company, and questions the economics of potential downtime if the competitor can't support the solution. "A product may be cheap to buy, but expensive to own."
>
> As he spends his time dealing with C-level executives in banks, he again underlines the comfort of dealing with a large, stable supplier. "Why would you buy a product to run your business from a company you probably wouldn't lend money to?"
>
> Shifting the issue from price to risk reduction, Gerry makes a lot of money selling his products, without having to reduce his price drastically to battle with smaller competitors.

Rarely is price the sole issue. You must look beyond the obvious to focus your energies on negotiating the right problem. Emotions are always at play. The buyer is concerned with actual and perceived fairness, personal reputation, self-image and relative negotiation achievements. The last thing he wants is to pay a higher price than his competitor, for the same product.

As real negotiation begins, you should extend the engagement framework you agreed with the customer during the sales cycle. You should have an agreed timescale for the negotiation and commit to a personal, fair and open negotiation process. Deepen your relationship further, before focusing on the numbers. Develop a 'social contract' – the spirit of the deal – with your customer. Because price is the most visible component of any negotiation, it will always receive the most attention. You job is to maximize the price. Where the buyer is looking for discount, try to change the package – not the price. Add something extra or deliver early.

Don't Confuse *Positions* with *Interests*

A *position* is a particular stance taken by one party in a negotiation. It typically outlines their preferred result. *Interests,* on the other hand, are the reasons behind the position. Interests define the problem. They are based on intangible motivations such as need, desires or concerns, which underlie the preferred solution. It is important that you distinguish between interests and positions. Your interests in a negotiation are whatever you care about that is at stake in the process. Complete Negotiators are clear on their ultimate interests, and those of the other side. They also know their trade-offs among lesser interests, and are remarkably flexible and creative on the means.

Simon is a sales executive in a software company that provides sales management solutions to the life assurance industry. A typical sale for Simon comprises a software license fee of $80,000, with an additional annual maintenance and support charge of $20,000, for a total purchase price of $100,000. Having competed effectively in a bid to a large insurance company, Simon was the preferred supplier. When it came to the negotiation, the buyer informed Simon that he needed him to sharpen his pencil a little, as he was only prepared to pay $75,000 in total. Simon was surprised, and a little dejected. He couldn't sell the software without maintenance, and there wasn't any way he could provide a full 25% discount. He tried everything to raise the buyer's offer. He offered free additional training programs to the buyer. He suggested that, if he could hold his price, he could add a second year's maintenance at a reduced rate. He even offered a dedicated support agent, just for that customer. It was all to no avail. The customer held firm, stating that he could only pay $75,000.

Simon was confused. This customer had been reasonable to deal with right through the selling cycle. He provided information as requested and gave honest feedback on issues and progress. Simon felt he was at an impasse. The customer wouldn't move from his $75,000 number – not one dollar. Finally, Simon just asked the customer, "What's magic about $75,000?"

The customer's response opened the door to a solution. "It's all I have left in this year's budget."

Though Simon had checked budget availability earlier in the selling cycle, a small project had been approved that took $50,000 from his buyer's coffers, leaving him with only $75,000. That left him $25,000 short, if he agreed to Simon's number. The buyer's issue wasn't value or price. It was that year's budget. His position stated that all he was prepared to pay was $75,000, while his interest, once uncovered, revealed that $75,000 was all he was prepared to pay in that financial year.

Simon solved the problem by selling him a two-year maintenance contract, and agreeing a payment schedule that met his customer's requirements. "Can you commit to a two-year support deal, if I structure the payment schedule such that you only have to pay $75,000 this year?"

Complete Negotiators probe beyond combative positions to uncover the shared interests that lie beneath. Arguing over positions is inefficient, and frequently damages the relationship between the seller and the buyer. Too much emphasis on positions drives negotiation toward a risky, ritual dance that does not meet either party's fundamental concerns. Learning about and reconciling the full set of interests requires patience, researching the other side, asking many questions, and really listening. When you shift the discussions from positions to interests, the path to resolution becomes clearer. When you focus on the buyer's interests, you can get to the heart of the matter more quickly, promote mutual understanding, and accelerate the search for a creative solution.

Understand BATNAs (Yours and Theirs)

BATNA is a term coined by Roger Fisher and William Ury in their 1981 bestseller, *Getting to Yes: Negotiating Without Giving In*. It is the acronym for Best Alternative To a Negotiated Agreement. It is your other option. Having a BATNA lets you know when to walk away from a negotiation without a deal. If the negotiation has arrived at that point where the deal on the table is less attractive than your alternative (your BATNA), you know that it is time to walk away. Your BATNA tells you when you should make that choice – it's the yardstick against which you should measure any negotiated agreement.

Sometimes, when explaining BATNAs, we use the analogy of not having all your eggs in the one basket. If you only have one option (and your opponent know that), then you have to take the deal at any cost. As the founders of Yahoo! are purported to have said, "**Y**ou **A**lways **H**ave **O**ther **O**ptions". You need those other options to be as good as you can make them. That's what having a strong BATNA is about.

More than that, however, BATNA is really the fulcrum on which the power of negotiation balances. If you are the preferred supplier to a customer, they have chosen you because you meet their needs better than any other vendor. If you walk away, they will lose something. Your BATNA is strong. Your negotiating position is strong. When the buyer has multiple vendors, who can offer similar products that don't seem terribly differentiated, then the buyer's BATNA is strong.

Sales executives sometimes feel that they don't have a strong BATNA. They think their walk-away position is weak and that the buyer holds all of the cards. As quarter-end approaches, the buyer knows that you're keen to get the deal done. But it probably doesn't make a difference to him whether the purchase order is signed at the end of December, or in the middle of January. For you, the sales professional, the easiest way to have a strong BATNA is to *not need* the deal. A full pipeline helps you get to that position. A strong BATNA turns your need into a want. Yes, you would like to close the deal in the current quarter but, if the buyer knows that you don't need it, your confident attitude will compel him to negotiate more reasonably to meet your interests.

BATNAs are not always readily apparent, and you should try always to determine the strongest one you can develop. Start with a list of options you have if you can't reach agreement. Evaluate each of these alternative options and then work to improve or enhance whichever option seems most attractive. Whether you are negotiating price, negotiating access to other buying influencers, or negotiating for information, you should always consider your BATNA. It points to alternative solutions, and strengthens your resolve to pursue your interests.

Your BATNA is just one part of the negotiation fulcrum. As you develop yours to be as strong as possible, you should consider the buyer's position. What's his BATNA? What options does he have if you can't conclude a deal? The more you can learn about what his alternatives are, and what he believes them to be, the better prepared you will be for the negotiation.

Listen Actively

Complete Negotiators listen actively. They ask hard questions and then pause, waiting for a response. Making sure that they heard correctly, they test their understanding and summarize what the buyer has said. Buyers like to be heard when they make a point. Consider using the Progressive Questioning Control Model to question and listen hard.

The cheapest concession you can make to a buyer is to let him know you are listening. Pay close attention to what has been said, repeat it, and use the knowledge to explore his interests, and deflect him from his position.

As you listen, you should maintain eye-contact with the buyer, focusing on what he is saying and how he is saying it. Try to remove your emotions from your listening so that you hear what is actually being said rather than what you want to hear. Your rate of thought will likely outpace his rate of speech, and you should use that gap to consider what key points the buyer is making. Is he stating a position, or giving hints pointing to his interests? You have the ability to listen, think and consider, at the same time, and all of these should be focused on ensuring that you understand what the buyer is saying. If the buyer is aggressive, listen while he speaks, and let him work through his issue. In this way, you lend little credence to the substance of his tirade while you learn what issues may fester if they are left uncovered.

Know When and How to Close

Timing is important when closing a deal. Poor negotiators either rush to the end-line or delay unnecessarily, afraid of failure. Both approaches produce bad results. Closing before the buyer is ready is perceived as pushy, and damages the relationship. Delaying allows time for further objections to arise. Complete Negotiators understand the how, when and where. They bring everything they need to the negotiation table in order to cement the deal, and they can isolate and agree a complete list of outstanding points of conflict, and resolve them one at a time.

As you strive to finalize the deal, you should try to strike a fair agreement, one that meets your goals and reflects the interests of the buyer. While it is true that the devil is in the detail, you should be prepared to concede minor points and give the buyer some wins, even when strength and logic is on your side. Don't let petty issues get in the way of closing the deal. Focus on your goals, not on winning.

Before you give a major concession, make sure that you have obtained agreement on what you will receive in return. "If I can find a way to package the products and services together to reduce your price, can you give me an order for three year's maintenance instead of one?" Notice that you have not given your concession until the buyer has indicated that he can do something for you. If you have determined that the buyer has the budget, upgrade the package rather than reduce the price. If he wants a reduction in price, suggest that you remove some component in the package. This allows you to 'call-out' the value of your offering once more.

You should never give a concession until you understand all of the outstanding points. If you do, the buyer may keep looking for further concessions as each issue arises. As you zone in on the final deal, reconfirm the buyer's commitment to your agreed timeframe. If you're selling to a large organization, help the buyer by providing him with a list of everything needed to close the negotiation. This might include a signed contract, designated company contacts, a credit report, his final implementation plan and dates for training. You may be tempted to begin to allocate resources to the customer to implement the project, but you should hold firm unless you have a committed order. Otherwise, you will weaken your position.

When you have addressed each of the points on the 'list to be agreed', ask for the order, close the deal and document the agreement.

PREPARING FOR NEGOTIATION

Before you begin the formal negotiation, you should prepare well. If you are a Complete Negotiator, you will have agreed a framework for the process, with your customer, setting out the defined scope and sequence of the negotiation.

Use the following questions to assist in your preparation:

- What do you hope to achieve out of the negotiation?
- What's your maximum plausible position?
- What's an acceptable outcome?
- When do you 'walk away'?
- What is your BATNA?
- How can you improve your BATNA?
- What type of negotiation do you expect: co-operative or combative?
- What are you willing to concede?
- What is the buyer's BATNA?
- Who are the people that need to be involved on the other side?
- What are the issues they care most about?
- What are the business circumstances of the deal for the buyer?
- What's the value to the buyer of completing the deal?
- How easy is it for the buyer to find a replacement deal?
- Can you document a list of unresolved issues?
- What are the logistics of the negotiation/closing?
- What emotional issues do you need to resolve for the buyer?

We have included a SELECT SELLING Negotiation Worksheet in the **Appendix**. It is also available to download in softcopy on www.selectselling.com.

CONCLUSION

It all comes down to this. You've worked hard at becoming a Sales Specialist. Your value proposition is crystal clear. You've become a 'trusted advisor' for your customers, and have disciplined yourself to work only on qualified deals. To maximize the return on your effort, you must negotiate well.

As with all aspects of SELECT SELLING, you must prepare fully before you enter the Negotiation Zone. Craft your strategies and tactics to engage with Smart Buyers or Value Extractors in the Value Tussle. To succeed, you must negotiate in all dimensions, recognizing that you can control the scope and sequence of the negotiation events. Your BATNA is a powerful tool. Work hard to develop the best one you can. As you do, consider the buyer's options, and work with him to reframe the negotiation. Focus on his interests and your goals rather than adopting negotiating positions. Listen actively to what the buyer says, and when you have addressed his issues, know when to close the deal. And don't forget, after the deal is done, when all is going well – ask for a referral.

Thanks for reading our book. We hope it will help you be more successful.

Good luck and good SELECT SELLING!

Donal Daly

Paul O'Dea

Chapter Summary: Memo to the Sales Specialist

- Prepare well before you begin negotiation.
- **Complete Negotiation** is a continuous process that begins at the start of the selling cycle.
- In the **Negotiation Zone**, you want your starting position to be your maximum plausible position.
- When dealing with **Value Extractors**, you have to know when and how to say "No". Don't negotiate alone; your buyer should be at your side.
- **Complete Negotiators** ensure that they deal with the right people, and negotiate the right issues, by having controlled the expectations and parameters of the negotiation, before sitting down to bargain.
- If you are a reticent negotiator, and you are on your own, pretend that you are negotiating for someone else.
- Embrace the buyer's perspective. It's not enough to know what you want from the negotiation. You have to understand what your customer wants.
- Before you begin to negotiate price, make sure that price is the only issue left to discuss.
- When the buyer is looking for a price discount, change the package – not the price.
- Don't confuse **positions** with **interests**.
- Always consider your **BATNA**. It points to alternative solutions, and strengthens your resolve to pursue your interests.
- Complete Negotiators listen actively.
- Before you give a concession, make sure you have obtained agreement on what you will receive in return.

APPENDIX

This Appendix contains copies of all the SELECT SELLING Worksheets mentioned in this book. Softcopies are also available for download at www.selectselling.com.

1. Sales Specialist Monitor Worksheet
2. Sweet Spot Indicator Worksheet
3. Customer Value Proposition Statement Worksheet
4. Combined Motivation/Solution Matrix Worksheet
5. Power Gauge
6. Progressive Questioning Control Model Worksheet
7. 4M Qualification Worksheet
8. Pipeline Creation Model Worksheet
9. Pipeline Analysis Model Worksheet
10. Sales Action Plan Worksheet
11. Negotiation Worksheet

1. Sales Specialist Monitor Worksheet

Review these attributes and consider how well they describe your competencies or attitude. Then score yourself on a scale of 0 to 5. The exercise should help you identify any areas of weakness in your sales proficiency and provide a framework for a self-improvement plan. For sales management; review these points for new hires, and decide for yourself what score they need for a pass grade.

		Measurement Criteria	Score
1	Value Selling	Can clearly articulate the product value to customers.	
2		Have clear understanding of why you win deals.	
3		Ask most customers for a referral.	
4		Follow a defined strategic sales process	
5		Ask why you lost a deal.	
6		Pursue only well qualified leads.	
7		Have a plan to differentiate against each major competitor.	
8		Have a plan to address most common objections.	
9	Customer Perspective	Viewed as 'trusted advisor' by customer.	
10		Can engage comfortably at most senior level.	
11		Have a deep understanding of the customer's business.	
12		Acts as customer advocate.	
13	Industry Knowledge	Can name industry influencers and understand their roles.	
14		Member of local industry networking group.	
15		Strong list of personal contacts in target industry.	
16	Personal Attributes	Refined questioning and listening skills.	
17		Good presentation, written and verbal communication skills.	
18		Motivated and confident.	
19		Have proven negotiation skills.	
20		Have strong business and analytical skills.	
		Total Score (out of 100)	

The supporting text for this worksheet is in SELECT SELLING, **Chapter 2: How to be a Sales Specialist**. If you need multiple copies, or want to revisit this exercise, softcopy is available on www.selectselling.com.

2. Sweet Spot Indicator Worksheet

Selecting your target customer accurately will shorten your sales cycle, increase the ROI for sales effort, reduce the marketing and support expenditure, and as a result, deliver greater profits. Answer these questions to profile your ideal target customer.

Sweet Spot Indicator	Answer
Industry Segment What's your target industry? Be very specific. Take into account 'external' factors such as regulatory compliance.	
Position on TALC What's the TALC profile of your target customer?	
Business Discipline Is your ideal customer focused on operational efficiency, product leadership or customer intimacy? How does your product help?	
Budget or Annual Spend What is the annual budget [range] you expect your ideal customer to spend in the business area to which your solution applies?	
Key Decision Maker Who in the target company is the ideal buyer?	
Key Customer Need What is the one, single requirement that you want the customer to be focused on in the context of your solution?	

The supporting text for this worksheet is in SELECT SELLING, **Chapter 3: Select a Customer Value Proposition**. If you need multiple copies, or want to revisit this exercise, softcopy is available on www.selectselling.com.

3. Customer Value Proposition Statement Worksheet

It is very helpful if you can create a short Customer Value Proposition Statement to articulate your value. This delivers the clarity you need, to communicate with your friends, colleagues and customers. Answer these questions to get started.

CVP Questions	Answers
High Level Description In 25 words or less, identify your market and describe what your company does for your target customer.	
Benefit Statement Outline the benefits that you can promise to deliver to your target customers.	
Customer Pain What is the compelling reason for the customer to buy your service or product? Describe his business problem or pain.	
Buyer Description Within the target company, you must be able to decide the profile of the likely buyer.	
Differentiation What makes you different? Why should the customer decide to do business with you rather than your competitor?	
Delivery Mechanism Describe how the product is delivered to the customer. Include reference to your channel strategy, your own offices or your partners	

The supporting text for this worksheet is in SELECT SELLING, **Chapter 3: Select a Customer Value Proposition**. If you need multiple copies, or want to revisit this exercise, softcopy is available on www.selectselling.com.

4. Combined Motivation / Solution Matrix Worksheet

It is critical to understand the motivation of each of the buyer roles. Some will have more influence than others, but you should take the time to discover the Problem as perceived by each buyer, the Cause and the Impact. The SELECT SELLING Progressive Questioning Control Model (see **Worksheet 6**) can also be used to help you uncover this information.

Buyer		Name / Title		Problem / Cause / Impact / Solution
LOB Manager	N		P	
			C	
	T		I	
			S	
User Buyer	N		P	
			C	
	T		I	
			S	
Evaluator	N		P	
			C	
	T		I	
			S	
Financial	N		P	
			C	
	T		I	
			S	
Legal / Procurement	N		P	
			C	
	T		I	
			S	
Internal Champion	N		P	
			C	
	T		I	
			S	

The supporting text for this worksheet is in SELECT SELLING, **Chapter 4: The Buyer's Perspective**. If you need multiple copies, or want to revisit this exercise, softcopy is available on www.selectselling.com.

5. Power Gauge

The **SELECT SELLING** Power Gauge is an easy tool to use. The chart below divides the sale into the four phases of the buying cycle. For each named influencer or role, you should record each time you have meaningful contact with each individual. Provide a name and title for each of the buyers, and tick the appropriate box when you make progress with that buyer, for each phase of the buying cycle. A quick look will identify gaps in your access to power.

Buying Cycle Phases ▶		Requirements			Evidence			Acquisition			Post-Sale		
	LOB Manager												
N													
T													
	User Buyer												
N													
T													
	Evaluator												
N													
T													
	Financial Buyer												
N													
T													
	Legal Buyer												
N													
T													
	Internal Champion												
N													
T													

The supporting text for this worksheet is in **SELECT SELLING, Chapter 4: The Buyer's Perspective**. If you need multiple copies, or want to revisit this exercise, softcopy is available on www.selectselling.com.

6. Progressive Questioning Control Model Worksheet

PQCM can be used to uncover requirements and understand customers' needs. **Discover** questions should be open and inviting. **Develop** questions expand your understanding of the extent of customer pain. **Control** questions show the customer that you have been listening, and that your understanding of his problem and perspective is correct.

Questions	Cause	Impact	Suggest	Action
Discover	What is causing the pain?	Who is impacted and how?	How can we solve this?	What's the first thing to do?
Q.1				
Q.2				
Develop	Is it because ...?	Is [Buyer] impacted?	What if we could ...?	When would you like to ...?
Q.3				
Q.4				
Control	So the problem is ...?	So the impact of this pain is ...	If we could do this, you think ...	If I deliver this, would you ...?
Q.5				
Q.6				

The supporting text for this worksheet is in SELECT SELLING, **Chapter 5: Discover, Develop & Control the Opportunity**. If you need multiple copies, or want to revisit this exercise, softcopy is available on www.selectselling.com.

7. 4M Qualification Worksheet

Qualification is not an event. It's an ongoing process. As buyers evaluate you, you must continue to qualify them. You must make sure that you question for objective and accurate answers. Use the **SELECT SELLING** 4M Qualification Model to qualify the customer, as well as to identify information gaps and potential areas of risk in a sale.

Qualifier	Comment
Method	
Understand all steps in the buying process.	
Understand competitive issues.	
Engage with the LOB Manager.	
Understand ALL decision criteria.	
Money	
Is budget allocated, authorized, available?	
Check for competing projects.	
Learn how the budget was determined.	
Check if you can win, and is it worth winning.	
Motivation	
Identify the personal pain for each influencer.	
Can you meet the need of each influencer?	
Agree, and document, the business problem.	
Agree the ROI model with the customer.	
Momentum	
What's buyer resource commitment?	
Determine the compelling reason to buy.	
Assess resource committed by customer.	
Understand the behavior change impact.	

The supporting text for this worksheet is in SELECT SELLING, **Chapter 6: Do You Qualify to Sell?** If you need multiple copies, or want to revisit this exercise, softcopy is available on www.selectselling.com.

8. Pipeline Creation Model Worksheet

Use this worksheet to list the Qualifiers, and to record the Pipeline Value Factor, or PVF, for each Pipeline Stage.

Stage	Qualifiers
Requirements	
	Requirements PVF Target Value:
Evidence	
	Evidence PVF Target Value:
Acquisition	
	Acquisition PVF Target Value:
Verbal Order	
	Verbal Order PVF Target Value:

The supporting text for this worksheet is in SELECT SELLING, **Chapter 7: The SELECT SELLING Pipeline Management System.** If you need multiple copies, or want to revisit this exercise, softcopy is available on www.selectselling.com.

9. Pipeline Analysis Model Worksheet

How long is your typical sales cycle? How much time passes during each phase of the buying cycle? To keep the pipeline balanced, and maintain a steady deal flow, you need to have an adequate number and value of opportunities at each stage in the pipeline. Use this worksheet to monitor your progress. How long is your typical sales cycle? How much time passes during each phase of the buying cycle? To keep the pipeline balanced, and maintain a steady deal flow, you need to have an adequate number and value of opportunities at each stage in the pipeline. Use this worksheet to monitor your progress.

Stage	Qty	$ Value	Account Name
Requirements			
Total R			**PVF Target Value:**
Evidence			
Total E			**PVF Target Value:**
Acquisition			
Total A			**PVF Target Value:**
Verbal Order			
Total V			**PVF Target Value:**

The supporting text for this worksheet is in SELECT SELLING, **Chapter 7: The SELECT SELLING Pipeline Management System.** If you need multiple copies, or want to revisit this exercise, softcopy is available on www.selectselling.com.

10. Sales Action Plan Worksheet

The **SELECT SELLING** Sales Action Plan helps clarify your thinking, lessens the chance of missing something, and forces you to build a realistic timeline for the sale. It also lets you share the project with colleagues, on whom you depend. If you are managing a number of accounts simultaneously, you've got to keep track of a lot of information.

Account Name:
Owner:
Pipeline Stage:
Date:

Objectives & Tactics	Resources	Date	Status

The supporting text for this worksheet is in **SELECT SELLING, Chapter 8: Implementing SELECT SELLING: Sales Action Planning.** If you need multiple copies, or want to revisit this exercise, softcopy is available on www.selectselling.com.

11. Negotiation Worksheet

Before you begin the formal negotiation, you should prepare well. If you are a Complete Negotiator, you will have agreed a framework for the process, with your customer, setting out the defined scope and sequence of the negotiation. Use the following pointers to assist in your preparation.

Account Name: **Deal Value:** **Owner:** **Date:**	
Negotiation Objectives	
Maximum Plausible Position	
Acceptable Outcome	
Existing BATNA	
How can you improve BATNA?	
Concessions	
Type of negotiation	
Buyer's BATNA	
Buyer negotiators	
Main buyer interests	
List of unresolved issues	
Buyer's emotional issues	

The supporting text for this worksheet is in **SELECT SELLING, Chapter 9: The Continuous Art of Complete Negotiation**. If you need multiple copies, or want to revisit this exercise, softcopy is available on www.selectselling.com.

GLOSSARY

Acquisition	See **Buying Cycle Phase – Acquisition**
Active need – solution vision	See **Three Types of Customer Need**
Addressable market	The total potential sales value for the year from your target market. It is equal to the total number of target customers (N) multiplied by the average value of the sale (V$) and finally multiplied by the percentage of customers (C%) likely to purchase in any one year [AM$ = N x V$ x C%]
Ambient Value	The qualitative value that a customer receives from a product – improved image. We recommend converting ambient value to measurable value (see below).
BATNA	Best Alternative To a Negotiated Agreement – your back-up option if the deal proposed is unsatisfactory. Having a BATNA lets you know when to walk away from a negotiation without a deal.
Buying Cycle	The four phases that the customer goes though in making a purchase: Requirements, Evidence, Acquisition and Post-Sales.
Buying Cycle Phase – Acquisition	The third stage of the buying cycle, where the customer is about to sign a contract and where risk and price become uppermost in his mind.
Buying Cycle Phase – Evidence	The second phase of the buying cycle, during which the customer requires very specific data to substantiate vendor claims that they can meet the requirements outlined.
Buying Cycle Phase – Post-Sale	The final stage of the buying cycle, where the customer is anxious to see the new product implemented and delivering the benefits that justify his decision to buy.
Buying Cycle Phase – Requirements	The first phase of the customer's buying cycle, during which he is concerned about his needs, wants and the buying process.

Buying Influencers	The six individual buyer roles that may be involved when a large corporation makes a purchase (Line of Business Manager, User Buyer, Evaluator, Financial Buyer, Legal Buyer, Internal Champion).
Competitive Differentiation	The unique, highly-valued, benefit that your product brings to your customers.
Customer Value Proposition (CVP)	The unique value that you provide to your customer. It summarizes the benefits that your product provides – it is your promise to deliver.
Critical Risk	The key risk that could cause you to lose a sale.
Customer Advocacy	A characteristic of a Sales Specialist. A customer advocate acts as a trusted advisor to the customer, marshalling his own company's resources and his customer's resources to ensure that his customer succeeds.
Customer Pain	The impact of a problem on the customer's business. Until pain (and value) exists in the mind of the buyer, any price is too high to pay for a solution.
Evaluator	The person in the buyer's organization who is concerned with how well your solution meets internal or IT standards. He is not concerned, necessarily, with business issues or ease of use of the product.
Evidence	See **Buying Cycle Phase – Evidence**
Financial Buyer	The person in the buyer's organization who is concerned with the cost of the purchase, as well as its impact on revenue, cost reduction or return on investment.
Funnel	See **Sales Pipeline**
Generalist	A sales professional who is bright, but ill-disciplined. He lacks market focus – going after all potential opportunities without selecting from his 'sweet spot' – and does not understand any particular industry in depth. He barely makes quota.
Internal Champion	The person(s) inside the buyer organization who will guide you during the sales process, open doors to the relevant contacts within the organization, and provide honest feedback to you on the buyer's perspective.
Irritants (Product Features)	Those elements of your product that annoy or frustrate the customer, but not enough to reject your product.
Known need – unknown solution	See **Three Types of Customer Need**

Lazy Gambler	A sales executive who has worked in the same company or industry for a long time. He lives off existing accounts or deals that just fall into his lap.
Legal / Procurement Buyer	The person in the buyer's organization who finalizes the detailed terms and conditions of a deal. His role is to protect the buyer organization's interests, potentially to the detriment of your value and margin.
Line of Business Manager (LOB Manager)	The person in the buyer's organization who has functional responsibility for solving a particular business problem and has general control over a pre-approved budget. He is the main contact throughout the sales process.
Measurable Value	Tangible value that the customer receives from a product – for example, 20% increase in customer retention or 10% reduction in production costs. Measurable value can be fully quantified and is easy to explain.
MEGOs (my eyes glaze over) (Product Features)	The features of your product that you think are really cool, but that customers either don't care about or don't like at all.
Method	See **Qualification Model 4M – Method**
Momentum	See **Qualification Model 4M – Momentum**
Money	See **Qualification Model 4M – Money**
Motivation	See **Qualification Model 4M – Motivation**
Negotiation Zone	The zone between a seller's win zone and a buyer's win zone. It is where the negotiation takes place and a deal will be agreed somewhere within it.
Pipeline Value Factor (PVF)	The multiple or percentage of your target you need in each phase of your pipeline to meet 100% of your target or quota in a given period.
Post-Sale	See **Buying Cycle Phase – Post Sale**
Procurement	See **Legal Buyer**
Progressive Questioning Control Model (PQCM)	A structured customer questioning process that helps you to understand the customer problem, determine its impact, jointly visualize solutions, and agree next actions.
Qualification Model 4M	A structured process that you can use to qualify the likelihood of the customer buying from you at each stage of the buying cycle. It identifies information gaps and potential areas of risk. It helps you align your selling actions to the customers buying actions. It consists of four key buying areas: Method, Money, Motivation and Momentum.

Qualification Model 4M – Method	Focuses on the need to understand the buyer's purchasing and decision-making processes.
Qualification Model 4M – Momentum	Focuses on the buyer's reason to purchase and implement a solution within a known timeframe.
Qualification Model 4M – Money	Relates to the availability of budget and other commercial aspects of the deal.
Qualification Model 4M – Motivation	Focuses on the buyer's personal and company reasons to purchase a solution from you.
Qualifiers (Pipeline Stages)	The qualification questions that determine where an opportunity belongs in the pipeline.
Qualifiers (Product Features)	The basic features that are a mandatory in a product for it to be considered a valid offering – for example, a steering wheel in a car.
Requirements	See **Buying Cycle Phase – Requirements**
Sales Objective	The next step(s) forward in the sales process, rather than the overall objective of the sales process. It should be SMART: Specific, Measurable, Achievable, Realistic and Timed.
Sales Pipeline (or Funnel)	The list of qualified opportunities segmented into the five phases of Target Customer Selected, Requirements, Evidence, Acquire and Verbal Order. The final four phases of the Sales Funnel are directly linked to the four phases of the Buying Cycle.
Sales Plan	The action plan you define to execute the sale. It involves carrying out the situation analysis, determining the sales objectives, defining the tactics to achieve the sales objectives, allocating the resources to execute the actions and, finally, executing the actions.
Sales Quadrant Profiler	Differentiates between the four different types of sales professional – Wishful Thinker, Lazy Gambler, Generalist & Sales Specialist – each with varying levels of product expertise, industry specialization and consequent levels of sales success.
Sales Specialist	See **Specialist (Sales)**
SELECT SELLING Power Gauge	A mechanism used to track your contact with each of the buying roles during the customer buying process stages of requirements, evidence, acquisition and post sale.

Situation Analysis A detailed assessment of the current status of an opportunity within the buying process.

Special Sauce (Product Features) The element of your offering that gets the customer really excited.

Specialist (Sales) A sales executive at the top of his profession. He always exceeds quota, is a customer confidante and is extremely focused.

Sweet Spot The customer segment in which your product offering best fits the customer's requirements. Your sweet spot is selected based on the customer's industry, position on the TALC, business discipline, likely available budget, position of the key decision-maker and the key customer need.

Three Types of Customer Need Unknown need – unknown problem: customer does not know that he has an issue or does not know that his issue can be solved. He sees no reason to change;
Known need – unknown solution: customer knows he has problem but does not know what to do about it;
Active need – solution vision: customer has an active need and a clear vision of how to address that need.

Unknown need – unknown problem See **Three Types of Customer Need**

User Buyer The buying influencer person/role that is concerned with the day-to-day operational issues of using your product. He will have to live with your product. His concerns are very personal and relate to the impact of your product on his job performance.

Value Extractors Buyer negotiators who see their role purely in terms of 'value denial' and price minimization. They engage continuously in the value tussle, using every opportunity to make you lower your price, or improve your offering.

Value Selling The practice of bringing value to the buyer as part of the sales process.

Value Tussle The battle between the buyer and the seller, where the buyer is trying to minimize his cost by denying value in the seller's product.

Verbal Order The final stage of the sales pipeline. It is the customer's verbal commitment to place the order with you. A percentage of verbal orders will not close.

Wishful Thinkers Sales executives who have a big forecast, have most deals at 90%, achieve minimal sales and get fired frequently.

INDEX

www.oaktreepress.com

OAK TREE PRESS
is a leading international developer and publisher of SME training and support materials, with an unrivalled range of content – in print, in software and on the web – for entrepreneurs at start-up and growth stages, as well as for enterprise support agencies. Its material is in use in Ireland, the UK, Finland, Greece, Norway and Slovenia.

In addition, **OAK TREE PRESS** is Ireland's leading business book publisher, with a broad list of business and management books.

◆

OAK TREE PRESS
19 Rutland Street, Cork, Ireland
T: + 353 21 4313855
F: + 353 21 4313496
E: info@oaktreepress.com
W: www.oaktreepress.com